TO:

....

FROM:

....

DATE:

....

The
Angel
Answer Book

ROBERT J. MORGAN

THOMAS NELSON
Since 1798

NASHVILLE   MEXICO CITY   RIO DE JANEIRO

Published in Nashville, Tennessee, by Thomas Nelson. Thomas Nelson is a
registered trademark of HarperCollins Christian Publishing, Inc.

Cover design by Greg Jackson, Thinkpen Design.

Thomas Nelson Titles may be purchased in bulk for educational, business,
fund-raising, or sales promotional use. For information, please email
specialmarkets@ThomasNelson.com.

ISBN-13: 978-0-7180-3251-7

Printed in China

15 16 17 18 LEO 5 4 3 2 1

Contents

Holy Angels

WHAT THE BIBLE SAYS ABOUT ANGELS

THE ORIGIN AND OCCUPATION OF ANGELS

Fallen Angels

THE ORIGIN OF EVIL ANGELS

DEMON POSSESSION AND POWERS

SATAN AND FALLEN ANGELS IN THE LAST DAYS

Introduction
All Night, All Day

When my friend Richard Hendrix was ten years old, he lived in the small coal mining town of Carbon Hill, Alabama. The Hendrix home sat on the edge of a forest and had a spanning porch where his mother and grandmother worked peeling apples or snapping beans. Richard loved to play with his friends in the nearby woods, especially around a large, overturned pine tree.

One day, as the family sat on the porch, a stranger approached. Since Carbon Hill was a small town, everyone knew the neighbors. The man, however, was unknown to them. He displayed Native American features and was toting a rifle. He asked if he could walk around and hunt snakes.

"Mama ordinarily would have told him to come back when Dad was home," Richard told me, "but for some reason she gave him permission. It seemed as though he belonged there; we felt safe in his presence."

The stranger walked straight down to the fallen pine tree as though he knew where he was going. It was a distance away, out of sight from the house, and no one had mentioned the spot to him. But a few moments later, the air cracked with rifle shots. Shortly, the stranger reappeared with three large rattlesnakes. The largest had twenty rattlers. He had shot them where the children would soon have been playing. The man turned and walked back down the road and was never seen again.

"We asked about him," said Richard, "but nobody knew him, and nobody in the neighborhood saw him come or go. If any of us had been bitten by one of the snakes, we wouldn't have survived long enough to get to the hospital twenty miles away. I've always wondered if it was a coincidence, or if we saw an angel without realizing it. I might not be alive today if not for this mysterious stranger showing up unannounced at our house that summer day in 1960."[1]

Coincidence? Mysterious stranger? Or angel? My files are bulging with stories like this, and many of them appear for the first time in print in this book. Some of these mysterious strangers are undoubtedly ordinary humans who showed up at just the right time in the providence of God. But I believe that others are angels, for the Bible speaks openly of their reality and activity in our world. Hebrews 13:2 says, "Do not forget to entertain strangers, for by so doing some people have entertained angels without knowing it."

This book represents a long-term effort on my part to understand the subject of angels in the teachings of the Bible and the story of Christ, in Christian and missionary history, and in everyday life. I'm not a speculator or enthusiast. I'm a Bible teacher devoted to "rightly dividing" the Word of God (2 Timothy 2:15 NKJV). There's no need to be fanciful or fanatical on this subject, for the Bible provides enough solid data for a satisfying understanding of these mysterious creatures. I'm not sure I've ever seen an angel, but I'm not sure I haven't. In these pages, I want to show you from Scripture and from a handful of first-person accounts what God's angels do—and what they do for us. As the hymnist said:

"All night, all day. Angels watching over me, my Lord."

Holy Angels

What the Bible Says About Angels

What are angels?

Angels are intelligent beings created by God as part of His spiritual realm. The word *angel* means *messenger*, and they were created to serve and glorify their Creator. The Bible refers to them as "ministering spirits," "heavenly hosts," and "holy ones" (Hebrews 1:14; Psalm 103:21; Jude 1:14).

Do angels really exist?

The Bible consistently affirms the existence of angels. They appear in its pages naturally, personally, and frequently. From Genesis to Revelation, the biblical writers weave angels in and out, and the teachings about angels are consistent and cohesive, rational and logical.

Angelology is a therapeutic subject for our souls. The Lord must have wanted us to ponder the marvel of angels if He spoke of them so frequently. Colossians 3:2 tells us to set our minds on things above, not on things of earth. The "things above" certainly include the angelic world. Martin Luther said, "The acknowledgment of angels is needful in the church. Therefore godly preachers should teach them logically. . . . They should show what angels are. . . . They must speak touching their function. . . . In this sort ought we to teach with care, method, and attention, touching the sweet and loving angels."[2]

British historian Thomas B. Macaulay described the Puritans as people "whose minds had derived a peculiar advantage from the daily contemplation of superior beings and eternal interests."[3]

What is the best true source for learning about angels?

We're curious about angels because angels are curious creatures. Thousands of books, stories, and speculative accounts have been written to describe their alleged existence and activities. But there is one—and only one—authoritative source of information we can fully trust: the Bible. Even the book you're reading right now is accurate only to the degree it presents the biblical facts.

The Word of God is our primary source of information—the only authoritative and infallible one—on the intriguing subject of angels. It's easy to take flying leaps of fancy on this theme, but what does the Bible say?

That was my standard when I worked my way through every book of the Bible, tracking down each reference to angels until I came to the grand crescendo of angelic activity permeating the book of Revelation. I found 234 specific passages about good angels and another 278 times when God is referred to as the "Lord of hosts" ("hosts" being the angelic armies of heaven). Angels are referenced in thirty-nine books of the Bible—nineteen in the Old Testament and twenty in the New—and the range of angelic activity spans the Scriptures from Genesis 3:24 to Revelation 22:16. As John Hunter put it, "We can as easily think of summer without flowers as of the Bible without angels."[4]

Why is the Bible our only accurate source of information about angels?

It's logical to assume that if there is a God, He is intelligent. If He is intelligent, He can communicate with His creation. If He can communicate with us, we would expect it to be a form of communication that is permanent, readable, capable of being retained and studied, filled with valuable information, translatable, and worthy of our time and attention. We would also expect it to be as trustworthy and accurate as God Himself, for He is its author. Why would an infallible God give us a book we couldn't trust? We would also expect this book to reveal things we couldn't otherwise discover for ourselves. God has given us such a book: the Bible. Psalm 119:130 says, "The unfolding of your words gives light." There are some things only

God can tell us, and He has revealed them in His Word. Everything else we read or study or think about angels must be measured by the standards of scriptural truth.

How are angels portrayed in the Bible?

As I pondered the teachings of Scripture on this subject, I was struck with how matter-of-factly the Bible treats this topic. The Lord doesn't try to convince us of the existence of angels or persuade us of their reality; He doesn't think of them as curious or bizarre creatures as we do, but as a normal part of His created order. In His world, angels are commonplace, a natural part of the environment. The biblical writers understood that there is a spiritual zone surrounding the earth where much unseen angelic and demonic activity exists. Famed pastor Charles Haddon Spurgeon once proclaimed, "I do not know how to explain it; I cannot tell how it is; but I believe angels have a great deal to do with the business of this world."[5]

In biblical text, angels pop in and out of stories as naturally as we'd drop into a coffee shop or duck out of an office. They're not mentioned gratuitously, and truth be told, it seems most Bible characters never knowingly saw an angel. Nevertheless, when needed, there they were.

What are some biblical examples of God using His angels to accomplish His will?

Angels comforted Hagar in the desert, delivered Lot from Sodom, guided Israel through the wilderness, fed Elijah under the juniper tree, surrounded Elisha with chariots of fire, saved Hezekiah from Assyria's onslaught, led Isaiah to spiritual commitment, directed Ezekiel into ministry, surrounded Jesus through every phase of His work, bore Lazarus to heaven, delivered Peter from prison, comforted Paul aboard a sinking ship, and gave John a VIP tour of New Jerusalem.

To believe the Bible is to believe in angels.

What do angels look like?

In the Bible sometimes these heavenly visitants appeared in human form and sometimes in superhuman splendor. Sometimes they were recognized as supernatural, but on other occasions they appeared as run-of-the-mill strangers. Sometimes the angels appeared in ones or twos; other times in multitudes. Some had wings; others didn't. Sometimes their feet were on the ground; sometimes they hovered in the sky. Often they materialized in three-dimensional reality, but occasionally they slipped into a person's dreams. Sometimes they were visible, but often they maintained their invisibility. In Revelation 18:1, an angel descended from heaven with such sunlike brilliance that the entire earth was illumined by his splendor.

We view angels as
supernatural beings, but
how does God view them?

After my extensive study of angels I have concluded that when God made the cosmos, He created many diverse life forms—fungi and bacteria, plants and animals, fish and birds, humans and angels. To God, angels are just as conventional as any other creature; they're part of the diversity of life that fills heaven and earth. They are interplanetary creatures who travel easily and instantly between dimensions of reality, between the spiritual and physical realms. They are virtually everywhere, even around me as I write this book and around you as you read it. They comprise our celestial family.

As we trace this theme through the Bible, we find angels treated realistically, but not paraded or flaunted. Their existence and enterprises are assumed, and we're assured of their concern for us. But they are never hyperpresented in Scripture. In fact, as my friend Dr. David Jeremiah observed, "Everything Scripture says concerning angels is in connection with something else as the main theme. There are no pages or passages whose central purpose is to spell out a doctrine of angels."[6]

To me, this is an astounding insight that subtly demonstrates the truthfulness of Scripture. If I were composing a supernatural book like a Bible for the ages—if mere humans were putting it together—there would undoubtedly be effusive descriptions and details of these divine agents. But God's Word is written with an economy of words and a logical consistency of method. Nowhere do we find chunks of Scripture singularly devoted to angels. Every reference to angels in the Bible is incidental to a greater topic.

What are some stories in the Bible that tell us about angelic activity?

Angels are active in Genesis, appearing in various forms at the gates of Eden, to Hagar, to Abraham, to Lot and the inhabitants of Sodom, and to Jacob. After Jacob, there's little mention of angels in the Pentateuch until we encounter the angel of the Lord, who accompanied Israel through the wilderness, and that "angel" was likely the preincarnate Christ Himself.[7]

- Judges has two prominent angel stories, and in subsequent books there are a few incidents involving angels in the careers of Saul, David, and Solomon. We also have another cluster of angelic sightings during the times of Elijah and Elisha.

- The Psalms give us a handful of precious verses about angels, though there are few references to angels in Proverbs or the other poetic books in the center of the Bible.
- Isaiah and Ezekiel had dramatic encounters with angels. The book of Daniel is full of angels, as is Zechariah. Few of the other Minor Prophets refer to angels.
- An explosion of angelic activity is connected with the ministry of Christ. Angels are involved in His birth, life, ministry, death, resurrection, ascension, and in the prophecies regarding His second coming.
- Angels occasionally showed up in the book of Acts with dramatic effect.
- There are sporadic references in the epistles to angels, giving us some intriguing hints and helps, yet no major passage in Paul's letters provides a systematic teaching about angels. We're given excellent information, however, in the book of Hebrews.
- The most intense concentration of angelic activity in the Bible is in the book of Revelation as it discloses their central role in

heavenly worship, in earthly tribulation, and in the victorious return and reign of Christ.

Angels were alive and
active during Bible times,
but what about today?

Angelic activity didn't end with the book of
Revelation, and the ministry of angels wasn't
limited to the days of the Bible. Angels continue
their nonstop work on behalf of the saints. Because
we have biblical indications that demonic activity
will increase as we draw closer to the end of the
ages, it's only reasonable to assume the same of
angelic enterprises.

When I was a student at Columbia International
University, my next-door roommate was Terry
Hammack, who, along with his wife, Sue, has faith-
fully served the Lord in Africa. Terry recently told
me of his friend Janet Schneidermann, who labored
more than forty years in northern Nigeria. She spent
many of those years alone in the town of Gashua

and was the only expatriate missionary within fifty miles. Much of her ministry was conducted against the backdrop of danger, and on one occasion she was warned by Nigerian colleagues to leave for a safer environment. Death threats were flying through the air like buzzards. Janet was a practitioner of Scripture memorization, and at the time she was committing Psalm 34:7 to heart: "The angel of the LORD encamps all around those who fear Him, and delivers them" (NKJV). As she meditated on that verse, she thought, *Thank You, Lord, for Your promise. Your protection is good enough for me, so I'm going to bed rather than leave my station.*

That night four men came from town to kill Janet. As they neared the secluded compound, they could see a tall man dressed in white with a sword in his hand guarding the front door. They were surprised and afraid because they had never seen a guard there before. They withdrew, and the next day they spied out the compound and questioned local informants. No one knew that Janet had hired a guard. That night the ruffians returned on the same mission. Again they were stopped dead in their tracks by this imposing guard.

The next day they casually "dropped by" to see Janet, feigning friendliness. In passing, they asked her about her guard. "I do not have a guard," she replied.

"We saw a huge man the last two nights with a long sword in his hand."

"Oh, him!" said Janet, laughing. "He must be the angel of the Lord that God promised to send because I fear Him." The men glanced at each other and hastily exited. No one ever approached her house again.[8]

What is the best verse in the Bible about angels?

As I worked my way through the 234 passages in the Bible on this subject, one verse stood out in neon colors, providing a set of basic definitions for this strange species of creature. Hebrews 1:14 says, "Are not all angels ministering spirits sent to serve those who will inherit salvation?" In my opinion, this is the best verse about angels in the Bible. This verse provides a definition of angels—they are ministering spirits. It reveals their essence—they are spiritual beings. And it tells us something of their purpose—they are assigned by God to assist His people.

Who are angels subject to?

You might want to put this book down and read the first chapter of Hebrews. You'll readily see the message that angels are subservient to Christ—made by and subject to Him.

When God the Son became human and took upon Himself the garb of flesh, He temporarily became a "little lower" than the angels He had created. Hebrews 2:9 says, "We see Jesus, who was made a little lower than the angels, now crowned with glory and honor because he suffered death."

Following His resurrection, Jesus resumed His full position and the prerogatives of His glory as He sat on heaven's throne, and the entire first chapter of Hebrews is devoted to telling us that He is as superior to the angels as the name He has inherited is superior to theirs (v. 4).

God the Father commands all the angels to worship Him (v. 6) and describes angels as "servants," while Jesus is referred to as "God" Himself, whose throne will last forever and ever (vv. 7–8). Which of the angels did God invite to sit at His right hand and rule with Him from the throne (v. 13)? None. Instead, "are not all angels ministering spirits sent to serve those who will inherit salvation?" (v. 14).

The idea of Hebrews 1, then, is that angels are created by and subject to Christ, who is both God and Lord. This is why angels hover worshipfully around the Lord Jesus in the biblical story, enveloping Him in His birth, during His ministry, and prophetically at His second coming. They gaze in awe at Him, and their example teaches us to love Him as well. They long to look into His work and redemption (1 Peter 1:12).

Are angels invisible?

Hebrews 1:14 also describes the "physique" or substance of angels. They are "ministering spirits." This accounts for their invisibility, their ability to travel quickly, to fly between heaven and earth, to hover in the skies, to surround the throne in heaven one moment while transporting themselves to a needed spot on earth in the next. That's why they can bridge the chasm between the spiritual and physical realms in the blink of an eye.

What does the Bible mean by the phrase "ministering spirits"?

This lies in the realm of mystery. Saint John of Damascus opined in the early 700s that angels were intelligent substances without matter or body. The delegates of the Second Council of Nicea in AD 787 avowed that angels had bodies composed of light. The Council of the Lateran in AD 1215 decided they were incorporeal, having no bodies at all.[9] Martin Luther said in the early 1500s, "An angel is a spiritual creature created by God without a body for the service of Christendom."[10]

John Wesley suggested that angels are "not clogged with flesh and blood like us," but might have bodies of "a finer substance; resembling fire or flame."[11]

Nevertheless, at times they do appear in visible form, and we don't know if their bodies are material or immaterial, temporary or permanent, real or perceived. Theologian Charles Hodge suggested that there is nothing in the Bible that "proves that angels are absolutely destitute of proper material bodies of any kind."[12]

Whatever their construction and constitution, angels have a great purpose. They are ministering spirits sent to serve those who will inherit salvation. Notice the verb *sent*. If they are sent, there must be a Sender. They are God's response to our needs. He sends them to aid those who inherit salvation.

Exactly how do angels serve those who inherit salvation?

The Bible gives us some clues, but many Christians can also speak from experience.

My friend Dr. Mary Ruth Wisehart told me of a time she was traveling alone to Spain. She's an independent traveler with a can-do attitude, but on this trip she was tired and unable to manage stairs. She was the last passenger to disembark from her overnight flight. Clutching two bags, she started through the labyrinth of passageways toward passport control. When she encountered a marble stairway with no handrails, she paused and told herself, "I guess I can make this." But as she stood at the top of the steps trying to visualize her descent, she heard a voice behind her speaking with an accent she couldn't detect. "Don't worry," he said. "I will help you." The young man had a backpack, and Dr. Wisehart couldn't see his face very well under his cap. Taking her bags, he helped her down the steps, then quickly disappeared ahead of her, running toward baggage claim.

Dr. Wisehart soon came to another stairway. She said to herself, "Well, I guess I can make this somehow." Suddenly the same voice spoke from behind. "Don't worry, I will help you." Taking her bags, he helped her down the steps; then he again ran ahead and disappeared before my friend could thank him.

"I don't know whether he was an angel," Dr. Wisehart told me, "but I think God sent him."[13]

John Wesley once preached a sermon about angels, saying that they minister to us "in a thousand ways which we do not now understand. They may prevent our falling into many dangers, which we are not sensible of; and may deliver us out of many others, though we know not whence our deliverance comes. How many times have we been strangely and accountably preserved . . . ! And it is well if we did not impute that preservation to chance, or to our own wisdom or strength. Not so: it was God (who) gave His angels charge over us, and in their hands they bore us up."[14]

For after all, are not all angels ministering spirits sent to serve those who will inherit salvation?

The book of Hebrews begins and ends with twin verses about angels. Hebrews 1:14 tells us what angels do for us:

They are ministering spirits sent to serve those who inherit salvation.

Hebrews 13:2 tells us what we do for angels:

In showing hospitality to strangers we could be entertaining them unaware.

What is an example of present-day angel activity?

When Merle and Gloria Inniger traveled from Pakistan to America, they stopped in London for a few days, and somewhere along the way Merle managed to lock the doors of the rental car and lose the keys. It was Saturday afternoon, and no locksmiths answered the phone. The rental car company said they didn't have a spare key.

Merle and Gloria panicked about missing their flight home. Two Christian friends came to commiserate, and the four bowed their heads and prayed for help. As they finished, they looked up as a strange man approached. He offered his keys to them. The man explained he owned a similar car and perhaps his keys would work.

Merle inserted the key into the door, but it was no match. On a lark, he walked around to the trunk. To his amazement, the key fit perfectly and the lid popped open. There on the floor of the trunk were his keys. They had apparently fallen earlier while he was taking something out. "Praise the Lord!" everyone shouted as Merle grabbed the keys. But when he turned to thank the stranger, no one was in sight. They looked in all directions, but the man had vanished. Later, Merle asked a locksmith about the chance of the man's key fitting his trunk. It was about one in twenty thousand.

"An angel?" Merle later wondered. "I have always felt he must have been."[15]

The Origin and Occupation of Angels

What does the Bible say about the origin of angels?

We mustn't think of angels yet as genies or errand boys who fly to our aid at every daily dilemma. The Bible provides a balanced perspective, and it's helpful to look at angels as Scripture does. What does the Bible say about the origin and occupation of angels?

Angels appear early in the Bible. Both the Old and New Testaments begin with angelic appearances right off the bat. The first angel in Scripture appeared in Genesis 3, guarding the path to the Tree of Life. In the Gospels, we encounter an angel before finishing the first chapter of the first Gospel—an angel appeared to Joseph in a dream, advising him to take Mary as his wife (Matthew 1:20).

Angels were present when God created the universe. Since they're created beings, they're not eternal in the sense that God is infinite. They were created by Him. But the Bible doesn't tell us exactly when they were made. Job 38:7 implies that angels were present at the creation of the universe, and Genesis 3:24 and Ezekiel 28:13–14 tell us angels were on hand in the garden of Eden. It seems that angels were among the first on God's agenda of creation.

What is the occupation of angels?

Angels exist to do God's bidding. Perhaps the best Old Testament verses about angels are Psalm 103:20–21: "Praise the Lord, you his angels, you mighty ones who do his bidding, who obey his word. Praise the Lord, all his heavenly hosts, you his servants who do his will." Notice the fourfold way angels are described: His angels, mighty ones, heavenly hosts, and His servants. Notice their threefold commitment to fulfill His bidding, His word, and His will. And don't miss the beginning of the verse: they are commanded to actively praise Him, to bless the Lord.

How do angels travel?

One of the most fascinating Bible texts about angels occurs when the patriarch Jacob stops to rest in Genesis 28. He was trekking through the desert when the sun descended behind the western dunes, and he found a stone to use as a pillow. That night, Jacob dreamed of an immense staircase from heaven to earth. The angels of God were traveling back and forth, ascending and descending. As hymnist Fanny Crosby put it, "Angels descending bring from above echoes of mercy, whispers of love."

When he woke from his dream, Jacob was overwhelmed. "Surely the LORD is in this place," he said, "and I was not aware of it. . . . How awesome is this place! This is none other than the house of God; this is the gate of heaven" (vv. 16–17). Science fiction writers often speak of a wormhole—a theoretical passageway or shortcut—in space. I don't know about wormholes, but Genesis 28 teaches that there are gateways between heaven and earth, and angels are constantly coming and going.

As we visualize the scene, we're prone to see it in slow motion: angels gracefully gliding up and down the stairs like hot air balloons rising and descending. But angels can also move quickly. In Daniel 9:21, the angel Gabriel was sent from heaven with a message, and he came "in swift flight."

How astounding to realize that we constantly live on holy ground, in the presence of the Lord and His angels. Look around right now. You can repeat Jacob's words as your own: "Surely the Lord is in this place, and I did not realize it. How awesome!" Whether you're reading this in your living room, at your bedside, on an airplane, or in a hospital or jail, you're on holy ground if Christ is your Lord and Savior.

Do angels ride horses while patrolling the earth?

When I began pastoring shortly after my college years, I chose the book of Zechariah as one of my first pulpit projects. In retrospect, it wasn't very smart. Zechariah is a mysterious book with a dizzying array of images, visions, and prophecies—not a good choice for a novice pastor. But I was drawn to the book, and I still am. Zechariah cracks the door into spiritual realms and lets us feel some of the invisible hum in the unseen dimensions around us.

In the opening chapters, Zechariah had a series of visions in a single night. In the first one, he saw an assortment of horses and horsemen among the myrtle trees near Jerusalem. When he asked about them, he was told, "They are the ones the LORD has sent out to patrol the earth." As Zechariah listened, the riders reported to their superior, "We have been patrolling the earth, and the whole earth is at peace" (1:10–11 NLT).

These were evidently God's Special Forces, an invisible team of angels who had been circling the earth observing the political and military activities of the nations. They were reporting to someone of higher rank.

Since this is a vision, we don't have to take everything literally. Angels certainly patrol the earth, but do they actually ride horses? I don't know. It's not impossible, of course. If the Lord made earthly horses, He can certainly create angelic ones. Whether or not the horses are literal or figurative, the point is the same: angels are constantly monitoring the activities of "earthlings" like us.

What are some of the biblical terms used to describe angels?

Angels are often described in military terms. They are called a "host," or army. The apostle John, in his vision of the second coming of Christ, wrote, "The armies of heaven were following him" (Revelation 19:14). The prophet Micaiah said, "I saw the LORD sitting on his throne with all the host of heaven standing around him on his right and on his left" (1 Kings 22:19). In Joshua 5:15, an imposing military general—apparently superhuman—appeared to Joshua on the outskirts of Jericho and identified himself as the "commander of the LORD's army."

In the Gospels, Jesus avowed He could have called more than twelve legions of angels had He chosen. *Legion* was a military term for a division of several thousand soldiers.

Angels are often seen with swords in their

hands, such as the cherub barring the way to the Tree of Life in Genesis 3, the angel blocking Balaam's way in Numbers 22, and the angel suspended over Jerusalem in 1 Chronicles 21.

In Daniel and Revelation, we're told of great wars and spiritual conflicts being fought in invisible realms. Ephesians 1:21 says that Jesus Christ is enthroned "far above all principality and power and might and dominion" (NKJV). Later we read these astonishing words: "For we do not wrestle against flesh and blood, but against principalities, against powers, against the rulers of the darkness of this age, against spiritual hosts of wickedness in the heavenly places" (6:12 NKJV).

Do angelic armies surround us?

As we'll see later, the demonic forces around us are more pervasive and persuasive than we know, but those for us are greater than those against us. A powerful throng of angels keeps an unseen vigil, and we can say with Martin Luther: "And though this world, with devils filled, should threaten to undo us, we will not fear, for God hath willed His truth to triumph through us."[16]

In 2 Kings 6, the prophet Elisha incurred the fury of the king of Syria, who sent forces to capture him. One night while Elisha was sleeping in the town of Dothan, the Syrian army silently surrounded and sealed off the city. In the morning, Elisha's servant rose, saw they were trapped, and ran to the prophet crying, "Alas, my master! What shall we do?" (v. 15 NKJV)

The prophet was calm. "Don't be afraid," he said. "Those who are with us are more than those who are with them." Elisha offered a simple prayer: "Lord, open his eyes so he may see." For a passing moment, the servant received enhanced eyesight that allowed him to view the unseen realm. "He looked and saw the hills full of horses and chariots of fire all around Elisha" (vv. 16–17).

Whatever our situation, we have an invisible army of powerful agents surrounding us and guarding us. We can say with the writer of Psalm 27: "The Lord is my light and my salvation; whom shall I fear? The Lord is the strength of my life; of whom shall I be afraid? . . . Though an army may encamp against me, my heart shall not fear" (vv. 1, 3 NKJV).

We aren't fitted with special-vision goggles allowing us to see the army of angels patrolling the world or surrounding the saints. Our human ears cannot hear the trumpet blasts, the clashing of swords, or the thundering of the troops. But the Bible leaves no doubt: "The angel of the Lord encamps all around those who fear Him, and delivers them" (Psalm 34:7 NKJV).

Which of the monarchs of the earth
Can boast a guard like ours,
Encircled from our second birth
With all the heavenly powers?
Myriads of bright, cherubic bands,
Sent by the King of kings,
Rejoice to bear us in their hands
And shade us with their wings.

—Charles Wesley

Do angels have paranormal powers?

In studying angels in the Bible, it's obvious that God's secret agents are glorious beings of superhuman strength and supernatural abilities. Adam and Eve were arguably the two best specimens of physicality in history, uniquely designed and personally built by God Himself. But in Genesis 3, they instinctively realized they were no match for the cherub with the flaming sword who blocked the way to the Tree of Life. The first couple didn't try to challenge this shining being.

In 2 Kings 19:35, a solitary angel wiped out the entire Assyrian army. It was the strangest battle in military history, and it changed the course of world events. Isaiah 37:36 says, "Then the angel of the LORD went out and put to death a hundred and eighty-five thousand men in the Assyrian camp.

When the people got up the next morning—there were all the dead bodies!"

It was an angel who rolled back the massive stone at the tomb of Christ as though it were made of Styrofoam. Additionally, the book of Revelation gives us one account after another of cataclysmic events unleashed on the earth by powerful angels in waves of judicial wrath and divine justice.

Angels are not omnipotent or almighty, as God is. There are limitations to their strength. But they are "muscular" beings, and they operate with the full authority of God as they do His bidding. They are powerful in dispensing judgment, but they're also strong on our behalf as they provide help and protection in times of need.

Do angels really watch over us?

Among their superhuman powers is the ability to watch us without our realizing it. The apostle Paul said that he and his fellow apostles were constantly on display "to the whole universe, to angels as well as to men" (1 Corinthians 4:9). When Paul instructed Timothy about the ministry, he said he was doing so in the presence of the holy angels (1 Timothy 5:21). Paul warned us to worship in appropriate ways at church "because of the angels" (1 Corinthians 11:10). Angels were watching over Hagar in the desert in Genesis 21, for example, and monitoring Peter's condition in prison in Acts 12 and Paul's on a sinking ship in Acts 27. No detail escaped their eye.

A writer from yesteryear suggested that many secret sins would be restrained if we simply remembered a fourfold reality: "When we are alone—it would keep us from many sins . . . [to realize that]

God seeth, and conscience within seeth, and angels without are witnesses; they grieve at it, and the devils about us rejoice at it."[17] In other words, God is always observing us, our conscience is aware of what we do in secret, and we are in full view of both angels (who are grieved when we sin) and demons (who rejoice when we fall).

How many angels are there?

There is strength in numbers, and the Bible tells us that the angelic population is virtually innumerable. Job asks, "Can his forces be numbered?" (25:3). I've already mentioned that Jesus had access to at least twelve legions of angels, "legion" being a division of several thousand men. He could have summoned a hundred thousand angels without even snapping His fingers.

The Bible alludes to different orders and ranks of angels, highly organized and managed, like a mighty military machine armed for the ages. Notice the interesting phraseology of Psalm 68:17: "The chariots of God are tens of thousands and thousands of thousands." Here the word *chariots* seems to be a synonym for "angels," and "tens of thousands and thousands of thousands" is a Hebrew expression for "innumerable."

When the prophet Daniel was allowed a glimpse of heaven's throne, he saw it surrounded by "ten thousand times ten thousand" (7:10). The writer of Hebrews spoke of "thousands upon thousands of angels in joyful assembly" (12:22).

At the birth of Christ, "a great company of the heavenly host" appeared in the night skies over Bethlehem (Luke 2:13).

In Revelation 9:16, John describes a swarm of demons ascending like locusts from the abyss during the Tribulation of the last days. He said, "The number of the mounted troops was two hundred million." If that represents only a portion of the population of fallen angels—and if fallen angels are only a third of all the angels God created (Revelation 12:4)—then the number of good angels must be incalculable.

The Powers and Personalities of Angels

Do angels have names and personalities?

In the Bible, we're given the names of only two good angels—Gabriel and Michael. That every angel has both name and personality is without question. When we read the angel stories of the Bible, we can easily see humor in some, anger in others, and compassion and concern in most of the stories. When they worship, it's with exuberance. When they battle, it is with determination. It seems that angels have emotions not unlike those we experience. Jesus told us they rejoice when one soul on earth confesses Him as Lord (Luke 15:10).

So angels have intellect, emotions, and volition. They are "persons" just as we are persons and as each member of the Godhead is a person. One day, we'll have a long list of angelic names in our contact lists, but for now we're told the names of only Gabriel and Michael.

Gabriel is the angel of the Annunciation. In Daniel 8 and 9, he imparts messianic information to Daniel. In Luke, this same character pays a visit to Zechariah and to Mary, announcing the births of John and Jesus respectively. His duty in Scripture was to prophetically pre-announce the coming of the Messiah.

Michael, on the other hand, appears in a more militant role. He is called an archangel, and we meet him in the books of Daniel, Jude, and Revelation. He seems to be the guardian angel of Israel, who engages in battle in the spiritual realms on behalf of God's chosen people.

Is it okay to worship angels?

Many people today worship angels, and some religions include the worship of angels as part of their rituals. Others may not consciously worship angels, but they become obsessed with angels' alleged presence or activities. This is wrong in God's eyes, for only He is to be worshiped. Yet it's understandable why we're tempted to render worship to angels. Even the apostle John nearly worshiped an angel as he received the contents of the book of Revelation.

In Revelation 19:10, John was so overwhelmed by his vision that he fell down to worship the angel. The angel quickly said, "Do not do it! I am a fellow servant with you and with your brothers who hold to the testimony of Jesus. Worship God!" Three chapters later, John repeated his mistake in 22:8–9:

I, John, am the one who heard and saw these things. And when I had heard and seen them, I fell down to worship at the feet of the angel who had been showing them to me. But he said to me, "Don't do that! I am a fellow servant with you and with your fellow prophets and with all who keep the words of this scroll. Worship God!"

What do angels have in common with Christians?

Revelation 19:10 is a startling description of angels. They are fellow servants with us. The Greek term is *sundoulos*. The prefix *sun* means "with," and *doulos* means "servant." In eternity—on the new earth and in the new heavens and in the celestial city of New Jerusalem—we'll be fellow workers and next-door neighbors with angels. We'll be serving the same cause and worshiping the same triune God. Nineteenth-century Scottish preacher Norman Macleod suggested that we'll discover on reaching heaven that God's angels are not strangers but old friends who have known all about us from the day of our birth till the hour of our death.[18]

For now, it's enough to know that our angelic "fellow workers" have the power to help us in ways suited to our circumstances—even if it means kicking us in the ribs.

What is my favorite angel story in the Bible?

One of my favorite angel stories in the Bible is in Acts 12. Simon Peter had been arrested by King Herod, who intended to execute him. He was bound by two chains in the Roman prison, and guarded by sixteen highly disciplined imperial soldiers. Sentries stood outside the cell. No Houdini on earth could have escaped.

Peter fully expected to lose his life, but that didn't keep him from falling into a deep sleep between two of his guards. The apostle's simple faith in Christ was a better comforter than the softest mattress or warmest blanket. During the night, God sent an angel to break Peter out of jail. It's hard not to smile when you read verses 7–19: "Suddenly an angel of the Lord appeared and a light shone in the cell. He struck Peter on the side and woke him up. 'Quick, get up!' he said, and the chains fell off Peter's wrists."

The angel told Peter to hurry and dress. Peter did so but thought he was dreaming or having a vision. "They passed the first and second guards and came to the iron gate leading to the city. It opened for them by itself, and they went through it. When they had walked the length of one street, suddenly the angel left him." Peter came to himself and said, "Now I know without a doubt that the Lord sent His angel and rescued me from Herod's clutches."

Meanwhile there was "no small commotion" among the soldiers as to what had become of Peter. Herod searched the prison top to bottom, then cross-examined the hapless guards and had them executed. Later, in his headquarters in Caesarea, while he was sitting on his throne and congratulating himself, another angel (or maybe the same one) showed up unseen by human eyes. Acts 12:23 says, "Because Herod did not give praise to God, an angel of the Lord struck him down, and he was eaten by worms and died."

Acts 12, then, contains two angel stories: an

apostle rescued from execution and a tyrant put to death. It pays to be on the right side of things!

The same angels at work in Acts 12 are still doing God's bidding. They are both our fellow servants and powerful spirits sent to serve those who inherit salvation. Phillips Brooks, the famous Boston pastor and the author of "O Little Town of Bethlehem," said, "I am sure that God and His angels help many a struggler who does not know where the help comes from."[19]

Sometimes that struggler is you or me.

Angels in the Life of Christ

In what seven great epochs in the story of Christ are angels prominent players?

First, His birth. There are six known sightings of angels connected with our Lord's nativity. The first was Gabriel's visit to Zechariah in Luke 1, telling him that he and his aged wife would conceive and bear the forerunner for Christ. Then Gabriel trekked to Nazareth to tell Mary she would be "overshadowed" by the Holy Spirit and would give birth to the Messiah. The angel appeared three times to Joseph in dreams, advising him every step of the way. We also have the spectacular scene over the fields of Bethlehem as the sky erupted in the greatest choir of angels in history, at least until Christ returns.[20]

We next encounter angels at the beginning of Jesus' ministry, at His temptation in the wilderness.

Following His tug-of-war with Satan, "the devil left him, and angels came and attended him" (Matthew 4:11). In those days, He "was with the wild animals, and angels attended him" (Mark 1:13).

The third time we encounter angels in the life of Christ is within His teaching, for He revealed previously classified information about them during His sermons. He explained that angels are genderless by nature. They neither marry nor are given in marriage, nor do they die (Matthew 22:30; Luke 20:36). He also told us they're not omniscient. There are some things they don't know, such as the timing of His return (Mark 13:32). Jesus told us that angels rejoice when people are saved (Luke 15:10) and that angels are travel guides, so to speak. They escort believers into heaven at the time of death (16:22).

Jesus also made this astonishing claim in John 1:51: "I tell you the truth, you shall see heaven open, and the angels of God ascending and descending on the Son of Man." He was comparing Himself to Jacob's ladder in Genesis 28. Jacob dreamed of a staircase stretching from earth to heaven, and he called the place Bethel, which means the "Gate of

God." Jesus was saying, in effect, "Jacob's ladder was a prototype or preview of Me. I am the connecting link between heaven and earth. As the God-man, I am the real Bethel, and I'm compassed by angels who come and go at My command."

We've already seen that Jesus could summon legions of angels at any moment, should He choose. Our Lord never gave a sermon on angelology, but as He spoke on other subjects, He mentioned angels. He always did so as though He possessed full knowledge of them and exercised full authority over the unseen realms.

Fourth, we have a plaintive glimpse of angelic activity on the night He was betrayed. Jesus prayed so earnestly on that evening that His sweat was like drops of blood. But Luke 22:43 tells us, "An angel from heaven appeared to him and strengthened him."

That strange and wonderful verse reminds me of a story in *The Ecclesiastical History of Socrates*, an early book of church history that documents the time from Emperor Constantine to the days of Theodosius II, a period of 140 years. It was written by Socrates of Constantinople, who was born in the fourth century. In his history of the church in Roman times, Socrates tells of a young man named Theodore who was subjected to cruel torture under the direction of Emperor Julian the Apostate. The young man was later asked about the pain he endured. Which was worse—the scourging or the rack? Theodore replied he was not able to answer that question, because during the torture a young man suddenly appeared beside him and, using a soft and cooling linen, wiped away the sweat, cooled him with water, and so strengthened his mind that the time of trial became a season of rapture rather than of suffering.[21]

Similarly, in the Garden of Gethsemane, an angel appeared to our Lord and strengthened Him. Yet with that one exception, there is a total silence regarding angelic activity at Calvary. Though He could have summoned all the legions of heaven, He died alone. It appears that for six hours one Friday the angels were told to stand down. We can only imagine their perplexity as they watched from afar.

But when Easter Sunday dawned, the angels sprang into action again—for the fifth time. All four Gospels describe the role of angels that day.

Matthew 28 tells us that as the women arrived at the tomb of Jesus, "There was a violent earthquake, for an angel of the Lord came down from heaven and, going to the tomb, rolled back the stone and sat on it. His appearance was like lightning, and his clothes were white as snow. The guards were so afraid of him that they shook and became like dead men" (vv. 2–4).

As the women entered the tomb, they didn't find it empty at all. "They saw a young man dressed in a white robe sitting on the right side, and they were alarmed. 'Don't be alarmed,' he said. 'You are looking for Jesus the Nazarene, who was crucified. He has risen!'" (Mark 16:5–6).

Luke adds that the Easter angels appeared to be two men arrayed in a startling wardrobe—"in clothes that gleamed like lightning" (24:4). Mary Magdalene saw "two angels in white, seated where Jesus' body had been, one at the head and the other at the foot. They asked her, 'Woman, why are you crying?'" (John 20:12–13).

Each of the Gospel writers tells the story from his own singular perspective. There's no evidence of collusion, no attempt to get their stories together. The differences in the details are not contradictions, just distinctions of perspective. The accounts smack of authenticity, as each author wants us to know one thing above all else—Jesus rose from the dead.

The sixth time we see angels around the life of Christ is at His ascension. According to Acts 1:9, Jesus was taken up before their eyes, and a cloud hid Him from their sight. The next two verses say: "They were looking intently up into the sky as he was going, when suddenly two men dressed in white stood beside them. 'Men of Galilee,' they said, 'why do you stand here looking into the sky? This same Jesus . . . will come back'" (vv. 10–11).

That brings us to the seventh epoch of angels in the life of Christ—at His return. Jesus will come in His Father's glory with His angels (Matthew 16:27). He said He would come in the clouds of the sky with power and great glory and with His angels (24:30–31). The apostle Paul declared that when the Lord Himself comes from heaven, it will be with a shout, "with the voice of the archangel and with the trumpet call of God" (1 Thessalonians 4:16). He will be "revealed from heaven in blazing fire with his powerful angels" (2 Thessalonians 1:7).

There's also the book of Revelation, where the word *angel* occurs more than eighty times. The angels mobilize during every phase of the events of the last days, and they will accompany our Lord's return to earth with shouts and songs and power and dominion. At the moment of His return, the choirs of heaven will burst into a hallelujah chorus that will reverberate through the entire universe: "Hallelujah! For our Lord God Almighty reigns. Let us rejoice and be glad and give him glory! For the wedding of the Lamb has come" (19:6–7).

Angels have worshiped and adored God the Son since the day He created them.

Angels Watching Over Me

What does the term *Mahanaim* mean, and what does it have to do with angels?

We seldom see our encamping angels, but they are on duty around the clock. Consider the curious reference to angels in Genesis 32. Jacob had decided to return home from a prolonged stay in Mesopotamia. Years before, as a young scoundrel, he had fled, having deceived his father and conned his brother Esau. Esau had sworn to kill him, and as far as Jacob knew, Esau, now a mighty sheik, still wanted him dead. Nevertheless, as God worked in his heart, Jacob knew he had to go home.

That's when we come to a cryptic passage: "Jacob also went on his way, and the angels of God met him. When Jacob saw them, he said, 'This is the camp of God!' So he named the place Mahanaim" (vv. 1–2). That's the entire passage;

there is no further explanation. But we do know that Mahanaim means "two camps."

Jacob was traveling with his family and a few servants, and they set up camp in the desert for the night. Apparently a band of angelic troopers was traveling alongside them unseen, and they too stopped there for the night. For a few moments, Jacob was allowed to see the contingent of angels encamped around him. How it must have encouraged Jacob to realize that God's angels were protecting him, conveying God's grace into his heart.

The "two camp" experience doesn't belong just to Jacob. It's for all God's children. Psalm 34:7 says, "The angel of the LORD encamps around those who fear him, and he delivers them."

Do angels take care of other physical needs besides our safety?

In the Bible, angels even provided physical necessities like food and water for God's people. When Hagar and her son were parched in the desert, an angel opened her eyes to see a nearby well (Genesis 21:19). When Elijah had a nervous breakdown, the angel of the Lord found him sleeping under a juniper tree in the desert. "All at once an angel touched him and said, 'Get up and eat.' He looked around, and there by his head was a cake of bread baked over hot coals, and a jar of water" (1 Kings 19:5–6). Talk about catering! This was bread from a heavenly bakery.

That's not the only time the angelic kitchens have been busy. For forty years, the angels provided manna for the Israelites as they wandered the desert. Psalm 78:24–25 says that God "rained down manna for the people to eat. . . . Men ate the bread of angels."

It's not impossible for angels to carry out similar missions today. Kenneth Ware was born in my native Tennessee, but after his father's death in World War I, his widowed mother returned to her homeland of Switzerland, and that's where Kenneth grew up. After coming to Christ, he felt called to ministry. He eventually married and sought to minister amid the chaos of World War II. One Saturday morning in September 1944, Kenneth and his wife, Suzie, awoke with nothing to eat and no money for groceries. Suzie decided to tell the Lord what she needed. "Jesus, I need five pounds of potatoes, two pounds of pastry flour, apples, pears, cauliflower, carrots, veal cutlets for Saturday, and beef for Sunday." Pausing, she added, "Thank You, Jesus."

At 11:30 that morning, Suzie responded to a rap on the door to find a man with a delivery. He seemed to be in his thirties, tall, with a radiant countenance, light hair, blue eyes, wearing a long blue apron over work clothes. "Mrs. Ware," he said, "I'm bringing you what you asked for."

Going into the kitchen, he emptied the basket onto the table, and Suzie realized the man had brought the items she had prayed for—no more, no less—down to the brand of pastry flour she had wanted. After the man left, the Wares stood by the window to watch him leave the building through the only exit, but they never saw him again. He just seemed to vanish.[22]

What are other ways angels bless us?

Sometimes it's not material provisions we need, but inner strength. When the prophet Daniel grew so weak that his strength was gone and he could hardly breathe, an angel touched him and gave him strength (10:17–18). While on a careening ship in the Mediterranean, Paul kept passengers and crew from despair by shouting this testimony over the howling storm:

> I urge you to keep up your courage, because not one of you will be lost. . . . Last night an angel of the God whose I am and whom I serve stood beside me and said, "Do not be afraid, Paul. You must stand trial before Caesar; and God has graciously given you the lives of all who sail with you." So keep up your courage, men, for I have faith in God that it will happen just as he told me. (Acts 27:22–25)

Even Jesus needed the steadying grace of His heavenly Father as conveyed to Him by an angel. Luke 22:43 says that in the Garden of Gethsemane "an angel from heaven appeared to him and strengthened him."

In Isaiah 6, the prophet Isaiah felt unworthy to assume his ministry. "Woe to me!" he cried. "For I am a man of unclean lips" (v. 5). In that moment of misery, God sent a seraph to reassure him of God's forgiving grace.

We can't fathom the ways that angels ferry God's goodness into our daily experiences. Peter used an interesting phrase in one of his letters. He spoke of "God's grace in its various forms" (1 Peter 4:10). The amazing grace of God—His goodness, gifts, blessings, and bounty—come in various forms and are bestowed through manifold means.

God blesses us each day with warming sunshine or replenishing showers, with twittering birds, with harvests of grain that provide our daily bread. He gives uplifting fellowship, inexhaustible answers to prayer, unfailing providential guidance, and the inner resources for abiding joy, patience, love, and hopefulness. This is the abundant life of

John 10:10 and the overflowing cup of Psalm 23:5. It would be surprising, knowing what we know from Scripture, if angels had nothing to do with administering God's grace to His people in their various needs.

Angels Deliver Us from Judgment

What do angels have to do with God's wrath and judgment?

On many levels, the biblical teaching about angels is interwoven with the truths of divine holiness and holy retribution. In fact, much of the information we have about angels is found in passages relating to God's wrath and judgment.

Angels are our worship leaders in heaven, singing, "Holy, Holy, Holy is the LORD Almighty" (Isaiah 6:3). They understand that God's holiness provides the moral baseline for the cosmos and that judgment is the natural consequence of evil. In Revelation 4, the angels around the throne sing a threefold theme, "Holy, Holy, Holy" (v. 8). Four chapters later, an angel hovering over the earth cries another threefold theme, "Woe! Woe! Woe . . . !" (8:13). Just as angels reverence God's holiness, they also pronounce His woe on those rejecting it.

As we'll see later in this book, Scripture clearly and consistently teaches the existence of a diabolical underworld of fallen angels—demons—who followed Lucifer in his rebellion against God. The apostle Peter said bluntly, "God did not spare angels when they sinned, but sent them to hell, putting them into gloomy dungeons to be held for judgment" (2 Peter 2:4). Jude concurs: "The angels who did not keep their positions of authority but abandoned their own home—these he has kept in darkness, bound with everlasting chains for judgment on the great Day" (v. 6).

Jesus said that on the great day of wrath, the Lord will say to those on His left hand, "Depart from me, you who are cursed, into the eternal fire prepared for the devil and his angels" (Matthew 25:41). When Jesus encountered demons during His earthly ministry, they begged Him not to torment them or throw them into the Abyss (Luke 8:31). According to the book of Revelation, the Abyss seems to be a sort of super-maximum-security prison in the underworld where the most virulent of the demons are kept until they're unleashed on the earth during the Great Tribulation. Afterward they will be forever consigned to the lake of fire, along with the devil and those who do his bidding (Revelation 9:1–2, 11; 11:7; 17:8; 20:1–2, 10, 15).

What role do angels play in dispensing God's judgment on sin-hardened individuals and society?

One of the Bible's earliest episodes with angels had to do with the cities of Sodom and Gomorrah. These towns had become so depraved that there was no goodness left in them. One day two angels arrived in Sodom. They looked like ordinary men, though we can assume they were notably handsome and well built. To put it plainly, the men of Sodom so lusted after these strangers that they wanted to stage a mass orgy and gang rape them. But the angels were on a mission, and the next morning they rained down missiles of divine judgment on the towns and their corrupt inhabitants. God pronounced the sentence, and angels carried out the decree.

In 1 Chronicles 21, we have this stunning passage: "God sent an angel to destroy Jerusalem. But as the angel was doing so, the Lord saw it and was grieved because of the calamity and said to the angel who was destroying the people, 'Enough! Withdraw your hand'" (v. 15).

Much of Revelation describes the waves of catastrophic judgment to be poured on the earth by angels during the Great Tribulation: "I saw in heaven another great and marvelous sign: seven angels with the seven last plagues—last, because with them God's wrath is completed" (15:1).

The apostle Paul wrote of the coming Day of Judgment: "This will happen when the Lord Jesus is revealed from heaven in blazing fire with his powerful angels. He will punish those who do not know God and do not obey the gospel of our Lord Jesus. They will be punished with everlasting destruction and shut out from the presence of the Lord" (2 Thessalonians 1:7–9).

Speaking of that coming Day, Jesus taught, "The harvest is the end of the age, and the harvesters are angels. . . . The angels will come and separate the wicked from the righteous and throw them into the fiery furnace, where there will be weeping and gnashing of teeth" (Matthew 13:39, 49–50).

The angels are God's military police, dispensing justice and keeping our universe from being overwhelmed by the flood of moral evil that threatens. They carry out His decrees, administer His justice, and will inflict His righteous wrath on the world at the end of history.

Do angels deliver us from God's judgment?

Just as a police officer protects the innocent while punishing the guilty, the angels are responsible for guarding those who are washed in the blood of Calvary. In the story of Sodom, the two-person team came specifically to deliver the one and only righteous family in town. They showed up in the neighborhood of a man named Lot, whom the apostle Peter later described as "a righteous man who was sick of the shameful immorality of the wicked people around him. . . . [He] was tormented in his soul by the wickedness he saw and heard day after day" (2 Peter 2:7–8 NLT).

Lot met the angels, thinking they were simply wayfaring men. Following the rules of ancient hospitality, he offered them a room at his house. "No," they answered, "we will spend the night in the square." But Lot insisted, took them home, and prepared supper for them. That night the men of the city, young and old, stormed the house to violate the strangers, and only the angelic power of the visitors shielded Lot's family. The next morning, the angels literally seized Lot's hand and those of his wife and daughters and rushed them to safety before judgment fell.

When I think of the story of the angels delivering Lot, I can't help but remember a similar story told me by my friend Dr. Warren Larson, director of the Zwemer Center for Muslim Studies at Columbia International University. In a town near the capital of Islamabad, Pakistan, a wave of persecution threatened the home of a zealous Christian named Qureshi, sometimes called "The Peanut Butter Man" because he makes and markets peanut butter. Local imams tried to force Qureshi to abandon his Christian faith, pressuring him with boycotts and bribes. Failing at that, they incited the Islamic villagers to surround the man's house and burn it to the ground with the Qureshi family inside. As the crowd swarmed the house, Mr. Qureshi gathered his family and tried to prepare them for the end. He reminded them that no suffering could be compared to the glory Christ would reveal. They prayed and sang and waited for the final assault.

Suddenly a voice, clear and sharp, spoke above the roar of the mob: "Do not harm this person and his family. He is a good man. Don't you remember how he helped build a road and repair your canal? Do you forget how he provided water for you when the village well dried up?"

The crowd grew silent. Then one by one people drifted away, until the mob had dispersed. No one ever knew the source of the words. Rumors spread through the town that angels protected the Christians, and Mr. Qureshi was able to continue evangelizing with New Testament boldness.[23]

Do angels appear to animals?

Scripture's most comical angel story is about Balaam. He wasn't exactly a good man—he was a soothsayer who eventually perished because of his sin. In Numbers 22, he was hired by the king of Moab to curse the children of Israel who were massed at the border. The Lord warned him not to do it, but Balaam decided to travel to the area anyway.

Early the morning of his trip, Balaam saddled his old donkey and the two of them went clopping down the road. An angel of the Lord suddenly appeared, blocking the way. The donkey saw the angel, but Balaam saw nothing. Startled by the sword-wielding angel, the beast bolted into the ditch. Balaam whacked her soundly and yanked her back into the road.

The angel reappeared farther on, this time at a place where the road squeezed between stone walls. The donkey veered against the rocks, smashing Balaam's foot. He angrily struck his donkey again.

The third time it happened, the poor donkey just collapsed under Balaam, sending him toppling to the ground. Mad as fire, Balaam staggered to his feet and struck the animal viciously. That's when one of the oddest miracles of Scripture occurred: "Then the Lord opened the donkey's mouth, and she said to Balaam, 'What have I done to you to make you beat me these three times?'" (v. 28)

Balaam answered the donkey, "You have made a fool of me! If I had a sword in my hand, I would kill you right now." The soothsayer was so livid he didn't realize he was in a shouting match with his donkey—and that the donkey was winning.

"Am I not your own donkey, which you have always ridden, to this day? Have I been in the habit of doing this to you?"

"No," replied Balaam.

At that moment, the Lord opened Balaam's eyes, and he saw the angel standing in the road, sword drawn. Balaam fell on his face. The angel asked, "Why have you beaten your donkey these three times? I have come here to oppose you because your path is a reckless one before me. The donkey saw me and turned away from me these three times. If she had not turned away, I would certainly have killed you by now, but I would have spared her" (vv. 29–32).

What is an example of a current-day rescue made by angels?

At a speaking engagement in Mississippi, a mutual friend introduced me to Velmarie Burton, who told me her story. Shortly after the birth of her third child, Drew, Velmarie had a visit from her pastor's wife, who delivered a pan of lasagna with a side dish of motherly advice. Pointing her finger at Velmarie, she said very directly: "You need to pray for guardian angels to protect your children from harm."

Velmarie took the counsel seriously and began asking the Lord to station guardian angels to protect the children. Another child came, and Velmarie developed a tradition of taking the children to Destin Beach, Florida, for August vacation. They always stayed in the same condominium on the ground floor. Because of the demands of the family's catfish farm, Velmarie's husband could seldom join them, so her mother or a family friend would go along to help with the children.

In 1993, the group checked into the condo, but this year their room was on the eighth floor. Velmarie slept soundly that Saturday night, but she was aroused from sleep the next morning by frantic banging at the door. She rushed to the door in her pajamas to find a man shouting, "Do you have a baby missing?"

Velmarie stared in horror at the railing of the balcony. Running to the edge, she looked down to see her baby lying motionless on the asphalt eight floors down. She later learned that while she slept, her older boys had awakened and opened the door. The toddlers had wandered onto the walkway and climbed onto a luggage cart. Drew had climbed onto the balcony and toppled over the side.

Velmarie reached the pavement just as sirens filled her ears. The paramedic hovering over the child shouted, "I have a pulse! Give me a backboard and oxygen, stat!"

The ambulance trip was a blur, but Velmarie will never forget the moment the doctor approached her as she sat alone, still pajama clad, in the waiting room. "Mrs. Burton," he said, "I have no medical explanation for it, but I cannot find anything wrong with your son. I want to do a CAT scan to check for internal injuries, but it appears he's fine."

The next day, newspapers across Florida carried the headlines of the toddler's miracle survival. *USA Today* carried the story, reporting that the child's diaper exploded on impact. Velmarie recalls one Florida paper ran a headline saying, "Toddler Survives Eight-Floor Tumble." She believes the headlines should have said: "Angels Protect Toddler During Eight-Story Plunge."

What is one of the most famous angelic rescues in biblical times?

One of the most famous angelic rescues involved the prophet Daniel, an esteemed statesman in ancient Babylon and Persia. Late in his career, his enemies arranged to have him convicted of a capital crime. Daniel was condemned to a terrible death—being thrown into a pit of hungry lions. When the covering was removed the next morning, no one expected to see even a morsel of the old man. But there he was. He had slept soundly, using the lions for both his pillow and blanket. He calmly told the king, "My God sent his angel, and he shut the mouths of the lions. They have not hurt me, because I was found innocent in his sight" (Daniel 6:22).

Why is it important for us to fear and obey the Lord if we want angelic assistance in our lives?

I n 1 Samuel 21, David was chased by the armies of King Saul across the border into enemy territory, where he was trapped by the king of Gath. His only hope was to bluff his way out of danger, which he did by feigning insanity. Later, in Psalm 34, he credited his escape to answered prayer and angelic aid. "I sought the Lord, and he answered me," he wrote. "This poor man called, and the Lord heard him; he saved him out of all his troubles. The angel of the Lord encamps around those who fear him, and he delivers them" (vv. 4, 6–7).

No angel showed up visibly, yet David believed his escape was facilitated by unseen angelic assistance as he feared the Lord. To fear the Lord means to reverence Him and respect His authority.

Psalm 34 is full of exhortations to fear and obey the Lord. Verse 9 says, "Fear the LORD, you his saints, for those who fear him lack nothing." The next verses tell us that fearing the Lord results in keeping our tongues from evil and our lips from lying. It results in turning from what is wrong, instead doing good and seeking peace. In the process, we have the fabulous promise of verse 7: "The angel of the LORD encamps around those who fear him, and he delivers them."

What is an easy verse to recall when in an emergency situation?

Psalm 91:11: "For he will command his angels concerning you to guard you in all your ways." A good way to remember this reference is to think of it as your 911 verse, with an added 1 because it works so well in extreme emergencies—9111, or Psalm 91:11.

In my book *Real Stories for the Soul*, I wrote about Charles Herbert Lightoller, a respected seaman for the White Star Line who was assigned to the maiden voyage of the *Titanic*. He was just drifting off to sleep on April 14, 1912, when he felt a bump in the ship's motion. Hopping from his bunk, he learned that the *Titanic* had struck an iceberg. As the horrors of that night unfolded, Lightoller found himself standing on the roof of the officers' quarters, helping women and children into lifeboats. He later said he would never forget the sight of the greenish water creeping up the steps toward his feet. Finally there was nothing left to do but walk, as it were, into the freezing waters of the North Atlantic.

The shock of the frigid water stunned him, and as he struggled to swim away from the ship, he was suddenly drawn back and pinned against a ventilation grate at the base of a funnel that went all the way down to boiler room six. As he was pulled under water, a Scripture came clearly to his mind—Psalm 91:11: "He will command his angels concerning you to guard you in all your ways."

At that moment, a blast of hot air exploded from the belly of the ship, shooting Lightoller like a missile to the surface of the ocean. He managed to grab a piece of wood but went down a second time. This time he resurfaced beside an overturned lifeboat and managed to pull himself on to it. Turning, he watched the last moments of the *Titanic*. Her stern swung up in the air until the ship was in "an absolutely perpendicular position." Then she slowly sank down into the water, with only a small gulp as her stern disappeared beneath the waves. About thirty men were atop the lifeboat, and together they recited the Lord's Prayer; then Lightoller took command of the boat and guided them to safety.[24]

Why don't angels always save us from harm?

There are times when we do suffer harm. We know by reading the rest of the Bible that God doesn't roll us in bubble wrap and pamper us all the way to heaven. The heroes of the Bible suffered, and some were slain for their faith. God's angels don't always deliver us in the way we'd choose, but always in the best way. We can take promises such as Psalm 91:11 literally, but we must leave the methods and means of their fulfillment to the Lord and His angelic servants. When we're in their care, how temporary our hurts! How permanent our blessings! The sufferings of this present life aren't worth comparing with the glory to be revealed. Our light and momentary afflictions are achieving for us an eternal weight of glory. Along the way, we have more protection from our angelic friends than we know.

Do we each have our own guardian angel?

The question "Do we each have our own guardian angel?" is the most frequently asked question I hear. This is a matter of great curiosity to people. As I recorded the story of Velmarie Burton's toddler, who plunged eight stories to the asphalt below, I thought of what Jesus said about children in Matthew 18:10: "See that you do not look down on one of these little ones. For I tell you that their angels in heaven always see the face of my Father in heaven."

Does this imply that every child has a guardian angel? Every person? Every church? The seven letters in Revelation 2 and 3 were each addressed to the "angel" overseeing these seven congregations. Since the word *angel* means "messenger," some commentators believe the letters were addressed to the human messengers—the pastors—of each church. But other commentaries point out that numerous other occurrences of the word *angel* in the book of Revelation refer to literal angels.

So are angels assigned to individual congregations? Do we have our own guardian angels? The early Christians seemed to think so. When Peter was delivered from prison in Acts 12, he went to a secret location where the Christians were praying for him. When he knocked at the door, the housekeeper was so excited that she ran to tell everyone without letting him in. Peter's friends couldn't believe he was free. "'You're out of your mind,'" they told her. . . . "'It must be his angel'" (v. 15).

My opinion is that these passages are interesting, but I'm not willing to base an entire doctrine of guardian angels on them. They just don't give enough information. We do know from the Bible that angels come and go. I believe they rotate on assignment. We have a host of angels watching over us. One of them very well may be in charge of us as our "guardian angel," and if so, I'm eager to meet mine in heaven. But I don't believe he does all the work alone. As John Wesley said: A convoy attends, a ministering host of invisible friends.

Can you describe an event when someone's guardian angel or angels seem to have made an appearance?

Reverend Edward King entered the ministry in 1854, in the English village of Wheatley. One night he was called to visit a dying man a mile or two away. The night was dark, but King trudged on by foot, only to arrive at the home and discover that no one was sick after all. He returned home perplexed.

Years later, when he was bishop of Lincoln, King made another visit, this time to a condemned prisoner under sentence of death. The criminal asked King if he remembered his useless nocturnal walk of years ago. "It was I who gave you the false message," said the man, "to lure you out that I might rob you." The bishop, curious, asked the man why he hadn't carried out his plan.

"I lay in hiding," said the man, "but when you came near, I saw you were not alone."

"But I was alone," said the bishop.

"No, you were not. There was a mysterious looking stranger walking close behind you, and he followed you to your home and then disappeared. My chance was gone, and I experienced a sensation I never felt before."[25]

As John Newton, author of "Amazing Grace," wrote in his hymn "The Believer's Safety," based on Psalm 91:

> Angels unseen attend the saints,
> And bear them in their arms,
> To cheer the spirit when it faints,
> And guard the life from harms.

Angels Assist God
in Answering
Our Prayers

Do angels assist God in answering our personal prayers?

Whether the Lord allows angels to eavesdrop on our prayers, I don't know. I do believe He frequently employs them in answering prayer: case in point, the prophet Daniel. As prime minister of Babylon and Persia, Daniel had a lifelong habit of retiring to his private quarters three times a day to spend time talking to the Lord (Daniel 6:10). On one occasion, Daniel had been poring over the writings of the prophet Jeremiah. He came to understand from Jeremiah's prophecies that the time had come for Israel to return from exile and once again repopulate the promised land. Daniel made this a matter of earnest prayer. One afternoon, the angel Gabriel showed up during his prayer time. "As soon as you began to pray," Gabriel told him, "an answer was given, which I have come to tell you" (9:23). Daniel made the request, God bestowed the grace, and an angel brought the answer.

In chapter 10, we have an even more remarkable story. Daniel was given a graphic vision by direct revelation from God. Deeply troubled, Daniel prayed earnestly to understand the vision. Three weeks passed. One day Daniel accompanied some men who were inspecting the banks of the Tigris River. Looking up, he saw a man dressed in linen with a belt of gold around his waist. His body was like topaz, his face like lightning, his eyes on fire. His arms and legs resembled burnished bronze that flashed in the sunshine. His voice was like the roar of a stadium.

The sudden appearance of this spectacular stranger drained the strength from Daniel's body like air from a balloon, and he collapsed. At once an angel stood beside him, touched him, and helped him to his hands and knees and gradually to his feet. The next words we read fill us with wonder. The angel said:

> Don't be afraid, Daniel. Since the first day you began to pray for understanding and to humble

yourself before your God, your request has been heard in heaven. I have come in answer to your prayer. But for twenty-one days the spirit prince of the kingdom of Persia blocked my way. Then Michael, one of the archangels, came to help me, and I left him there with the spirit prince of the kingdom of Persia. Now I am here to explain what will happen to your people in the future. (10:12–14 NLT)

No further explanation is given, but taken at face value, it appears that at the moment Daniel began praying, the answer was issued without delay, just as in the previous chapter. But powerful demonic forces had blocked the pathway of the angel bearing the answer. The impasse lasted a full three weeks until the archangel Michael arrived on the scene with his superior authority. The standoff was ended, and the delayed angel sped on to Daniel with the answer to his prayer.

Do angels face resistance when delivering answers to our prayers?

I'm staggered to know that there is so much invisible static in the unseen spheres. It's remarkable to think that our prayers to God and His answers to us may pass through the territory of the "prince of the power of the air" (Ephesians 2:2 NKJV). It's sobering to know that angels bearing the answers to our prayers are opposed and sometimes delayed by what Paul called "the rulers . . . the authorities . . . the spiritual forces of evil in the heavenly realms" (6:12). There's an invisible grid around our planet where unseen forces deploy. How thankful we should be for every answer to prayer that comes to us from day to day.

If angels deliver answers
to our prayers, why not
simply pray to them?

Nowhere does the Bible suggest we're to pray to angels. In fact, Paul warned the Colossians not to be deceived by anyone veering off into the worship of angels (2:18). Even though some of the biblical characters spoke to angels, there's no indication in Scripture that we're to offer prayers to them. But they do seem to play a role in the process of prayer, especially as they assist God in the delivery of His answers to our earnest petitions.

Is there an example of how angels might be mobilized in modern times to assist God in answering prayer?

Terry Hammack, who lived next door to me in college, has worked for the Lord in Nigeria for many years. Some time ago, when he and his wife, Sue, were stateside, they told me about the riots that broke out in the northern city of Kano in October of 1991. The trouble had started when a German evangelist announced a series of open-air evangelistic meetings in the area. This triggered a violent reaction by the Muslim population. Christian businesses and churches were targeted for looting and destruction, and believers found themselves in grave danger. Terry was able to evacuate his family to safety, but since he operated the communications equipment, he felt he should stay alongside the national leader, Pastor Garba.

On Tuesday morning, thousands of rioters surrounded the mission, wanting to burn it and the hospital to the ground. Pastor Garba met the crowd at the gate in a flowing traditional gown. He tried to reason with the mob, but the eyes of many seemed focused on an open space in the courtyard behind him, as though they saw something that startled them.

The mob moved down the street, but rumors began flying around town that the mission was on fire. One Muslim leader, who had paid a deposit for his wife to give birth at the mission hospital, showed up to see if he had lost his money. He reported fires burning on top of the walls and buildings, which prevented him from entering. But the fires didn't appear to be normal, and the buildings weren't consumed. He went home and called other religious men to view the phenomenon. They all saw the fires, which burned all day Tuesday, Wednesday, and Thursday.

Throughout those days, Terry and his compatriots, trapped inside the walls, expected an attack, but none came. "Though Pastor Garba and I engaged in prayer walks of protection around the walls during those days," he said, "we ourselves did not see the fires. But later, our coworker Janet Schneidermann, hearing the story, reminded us of Zechariah 2:5: "'And I myself will be a wall of fire around it,' declares the Lord, 'and I will be its glory within.'"[26]

There's more activity in the heavenly realms than we realize, and angels have more to do with answering our prayers than we know. As Martin Luther once quipped, the angels have long arms. They stand in the presence of God, yet reach you and me in our times of need.

Do angels sing?

Some writers have questioned whether angels actually sing, and this is a valid discussion. But I cannot imagine tuneless angels. God loves music. He filled the Bible with hymns. He filled the universe with singing creatures—from songbirds to giant blue whales. He puts songs in our mouths and melodies in our hearts. Can we really believe there's no music around the throne, that angels are somehow excluded from God's singing creation?

It's true that the verbs used for angelic communication are usually words like *said* and *called*, but those words don't exclude the medium of song. Who can imagine the night skies over Bethlehem filled with a host of choiring angels who weren't able to sing? Revelation is packed with hymns, so it's reasonable to assume they were sung. Does anyone really think their praise is rendered in a monotone?

Revelation 5:8–11 tells us that the twenty-four elders (who perhaps represent the raptured church) and the four living creatures (who seem to be cherubim-like angelic creatures) all had harps, "and they sang a new song" to the Lamb (v. 9). Verses 11–12 say, "Then I looked and heard the voice of many angels, numbering thousands upon thousands, and ten thousand times ten thousand. They encircled the throne and the living creatures and the elders. In a loud voice they sang: 'Worthy is the Lamb.'" Verse 13 goes on to say: "Then I heard every creature in heaven and on earth and under the earth and on the sea, and all that is in them, singing."[27]

Psalm 148:2 declares, "Praise him, all his angels, praise him, all his heavenly hosts." According to Hebrews 12:22, the presence of God is surrounded by "thousands upon thousands of angels in joyful assembly."

British hymnist Reginald Heber composed one of the greatest anthems of Christendom: "Holy, Holy, Holy." The second verse refers to two distinct categories of worshiping angels:

Cherubim and seraphim falling down before
Thee, who was, and is, and evermore shall be.

Who are seraphim?

Seraphim are a rank or species of angels mentioned only once in Scripture, when the prophet Isaiah was ordained to the ministry. In chapter 6, Isaiah testified:

> I saw the Lord seated on a throne, high and exalted, and the train of his robe filled the temple. Above him were seraphs, each with six wings: With two wings they covered their faces, with two they covered their feet, and with two they were flying. And they were calling to one another: "Holy, holy, holy is the Lord Almighty; the whole earth is full of his glory." At the sound of their voices the doorposts and thresholds shook and the temple was filled with smoke.

> "Woe to me!" I cried. "I am ruined! For I am a man of unclean lips." . . .

Then one of the seraphs flew to me with a live coal in his hand, which he had taken with tongs from the altar. With it he touched my mouth and said, "See, this has touched your lips; your guilt is taken away and your sin is atoned for."

Then I heard the voice of the Lord saying, "Whom shall I send? And who will go for us?" And I said, "Here am I. Send me!" (vv. 1–8)

Seraphs and *seraphim* probably come from an ancient Hebrew verb meaning "to burn." If so, we could describe seraphim as "burning ones" or "fiery ones." These six-winged creatures are both awesome and awestruck, both holy and humble, able to fly and capable of speaking. Their praise shook the temple to its foundations. They conveyed to Isaiah an assurance of God's grace and buttressed him as he surrendered himself fully to the ministry to which God was calling him.

Who are cherubim?

Whereas seraphim are mentioned only once in the Bible, cherubim are mentioned eighty-nine times. The first angels we encounter in the Bible are cherubim, whose flashing swords guarded the way to the tree of life (Genesis 3:24).

Several years ago, I delved into what the Bible says about the Old Testament tabernacle, the elaborate tent Moses constructed as a worship center in the wilderness. Incredibly, the Bible devotes fifty chapters to the tabernacle, and its every aspect points prophetically toward Christ Jesus. One of the things that surprised me was the preponderance of cherubim. Images of this strange variety of angel were everywhere. They showed up in carvings, statues, engravings, and embroideries, including the two great cherubim that loomed over the ark of the covenant in the Most Holy Place.

Isaiah 37:16 describes God as the "Lord Almighty . . . enthroned between the cherubim."

When Solomon built the temple as a permanent replacement for the well-worn tabernacle, he followed the same plan. Cherubim were all over the place. "In the inner sanctuary he made a pair of cherubim of olive wood. . . . On the walls all around the temple . . . he carved cherubim. . . . On the two olive wood doors he carved cherubim. . . . He also made two pine doors. . . . He carved cherubim . . . on them" (1 Kings 6:23, 29, 32, 34–35).

Why are there so many cherubim in the tabernacle and the temple?

I'll propose two reasons: First, the Holy Place in the temple was filled with images of angels because it was the localized, earthly representation of the true and eternal throne of God in heaven, which is surrounded by angels. Second, the presence of these cherubim reminded the priests and worshipers that as they approached the throne of almighty God, they were at that moment in the presence of an invisible multitude of holy angels hovering around them.

Can you imagine being Israel's high priest, entering this cube-shaped chamber once a year—the Holy of Holies? Positioned at the far end of the room sat a gilded chest known as the ark of the covenant, and over it towered two golden cherubim, their wings flying upward. It would visually remind you that you had just entered the ethereal presence of Almighty God and that you were surrounded on every side by actual cherubim—and who knows how many!

That's worship! Whenever we approach the throne of grace, we're coming into the presence of Him who is thrice holy, and we're joining the heavenly hosts hovering near. Together—you and me, the cherubim and seraphim and all the angels, the seen and the unseen—we join in praising Him who was and is and evermore shall be. That's what happens as we worship, both privately and with others.

The Bible says,

> "Since we have confidence to enter the Most Holy Place by the blood of Jesus, by a new and living way opened for us through the curtain, that is, his body, and since we have a great priest over the house of God, let us draw near to God with a sincere heart in full assurance of faith" (Hebrews 10:19–22).

How will angels be involved in the second coming of Christ?

When we come to the book of Revelation, we meet a set of angelic creatures who closely resemble Ezekiel's cherubim. The apostle John, writing in Revelation 4, said:

> In the center, around the throne, were four living creatures, and they were covered with eyes, in front and in back. The first living creature was like a lion, the second was like an ox, the third had a face like a man, the fourth was like a flying eagle. Each of the four living creatures had six wings and was covered with eyes all around, even under his wings. Day and night they never stop saying: "Holy, holy, holy is the Lord God Almighty, who was, and is, and is to come." (vv. 6–8)

Verses 9–11 go on to say:

Whenever the living creatures give glory, honor and thanks to him who sits on the throne and who lives for ever and ever, the twenty-four elders fall down before him who sits on the throne, and worship him who lives for ever and ever. They lay their crowns before the throne and say: "You are worthy, our Lord and God, to receive glory and honor and power; for you created all things, and by your will they were created and have their being."

If, as some expositors believe, the church has been raptured at this point in the book of Revelation, the twenty-four elders may represent the church of all the ages. If so, Revelation 4 offers a resplendent picture of angels leading Christians in thunderous worship around the throne in the New Jerusalem as the world below braces for the Great Tribulation to be unleashed in Revelation 6–18.

In Revelation 19, as Christ prepares to come to earth again at the moment of the Second Coming, all of heaven erupts in worship, led by the angels: "Hallelujah! For our Lord God Almighty reigns. Let us rejoice and be glad and give Him glory!" (vv. 6–7)

How much we could learn about worship if, as we read through the Bible, we noticed how God's seraphim and cherubim worship Him, along with all the heavenly hosts! Perhaps these passages will whet our appetites. I don't know about you, but I'm not a gifted singer. I can't seem to hit the right tones or sustain a clear note. My mind wanders during songs at church. My spirit sometimes sags even while listening to rousing Christian music or beautifully spoken prayers. Some days I crawl into bed feeling that I've not been a very active worshiper that day.

But it helps to imagine the ceiling parting enough to reveal—by faith—an echo of praise from around the throne. We can picture cherubim and seraphim falling down before God. We can see His angelic choirs hovering around the enthroned Trinity, sometimes soaring through the skies, sometimes falling on their faces, sometimes directing the music, sometimes singing alongside our loved ones who have gone on before, sometimes punctuating their praise with outbursts of "Hallelujah!"

Angels Usher
Us to Heaven

Do angels usher us to heaven when we die?

Yes. The Bible indicates this, and we have many deathbed experiences of dying saints that cannot be otherwise explained. Here's one example from my own experience:

Mrs. Agnes Frazier was the oldest member of our church and a woman of deep piety and enthusiastic spirituality. At age ninety-five, her health failed, and I received a call.

"Mrs. Agnes is asking for you," her nurse said. When I entered her room, she was almost too weak to look up at me. Her words were indistinct at times, but it soon became clear that she wanted to see me because she was curious about "these men."

"What men?" I asked.

"I keep seeing these two men."

"What do they look like?"

"Two men, dressed in white from head to foot, are standing at the end of my bed. I don't know what to tell them. What should I say if they ask me something?"

"Tell them," I said at length, "that you belong to Jesus."

That seemed to satisfy her. "Yes," she said, "I'll tell them I belong to Jesus." Shortly after, she fell asleep in Christ, and those two angels, I believe, ushered her to heaven.

One of the most reassuring words on this subject comes from the lips of our Lord Jesus. In Luke 16, He told the story of a beggar named Lazarus who suffered from a loathsome skin disease and from abject poverty. This poor man ate from the garbage while dogs licked his sores. But Jesus said, "The time came when the beggar died and the angels carried him to Abraham's side" (v. 22).

Notice that *angels* is plural. Commentator Matthew Henry suggested that one angel could surely have done the job, but the Lord sent an entire convoy, for saints should be escorted home not only in safety but also with honor.

The Greek word used here for *carry* can mean to lead, take away, carry, or transfer. It implies a sufficient means of transport from one place to another.

The phrase "Abraham's side" is meant to show us that this man, Lazarus, who was a wretched beggar on earth, soon found himself walking around with Abraham, Isaac, Jacob, and all the great heroes of God who had arrived in heaven before him. It suggests literal, conscious fellowship with our friends in paradise. In Matthew 8:11, Jesus used similar language in speaking of the joy of going to be with Abraham, Isaac, and Jacob.

Luke 16:22 signifies a precious promise for all of us who occasionally worry about the moment of death. It reassures us we have nothing to fear, for Christ has paved the way, and the angels will see to it that we don't make the trip alone.

Are there other biblical examples of angels escorting people to heaven at the end of their earthly lives?

In 2 Kings 2, the prophet Elijah came to the end of his earthly duties, and God decided to call him home to heaven. As he and his disciple, Elisha, were walking along in a remote area, their conversation was cut short. Suddenly "a chariot of fire and horses of fire appeared and separated the two of them, and Elijah went up to heaven in a whirlwind. Elisha saw this and cried out, 'My father! My father! The chariots and horsemen of Israel!' And Elisha saw him no more" (vv. 11–12).

It's true that Elijah didn't die, but it's equally true that the angels ushered him to heaven in dramatic fashion. That seems to be part of their job description—to escort us from this world to the next at the end of our earthly tour of duty.

What about when Jesus returns? What will the angels do then?

At the end of the age when the Lord Jesus returns for His people, He'll snatch us to heaven, and the angels will assist as escorts and ushers. Speaking about His return, Jesus said, "He will send his angels with a loud trumpet call, and they will gather his elect from the four winds, from one end of the heavens to the other" (Matthew 24:31).

In Revelation 21 and 22, an angel gave the apostle John a tour of the New Jerusalem. He showed him the city from a distance, then up close; then he accompanied him through the gates, down the golden street, and to the very center of the city with its crystal river, broad park, and glorious throne. If an angel served as the tour guide for John, it seems sensible that angels will be our orientation guides when we, too, arrive in the celestial city.

Our angel friends transport blessings to our lives, deliver us from judgment, protect us from danger, guide us through life, assist God in answering our prayers, teach us to worship, and usher us to heaven. And that's merely the beginning! Just think of the fun we're going to have with them in eternity!

How can I best prepare for the time when my earthly life will draw to a close?

The Lord Jesus spoke frequently about angels, but perhaps His soberest words are found in Luke 12:8–9: "I tell you, whoever acknowledges me before men, the Son of Man will also acknowledge him before the angels of God. But he who disowns me before men will be disowned before the angels of God."

He was telling us that there is a God, an eternity, a heaven and hell, powerful contingents of both angels and demons, and a day of eternal reckoning.

Angels, according to Hebrews 1:14, are sent to serve those who inherit salvation. Salvation is what Christ Jesus came to provide. It's the Lord Jesus Christ Himself, not angels, who can forgive our sins and give us eternal life. He is God "now in flesh appearing," the Savior who lived a righteous life, died on Calvary's cross, and rose from a Judean tomb—all for us. "Salvation is found in no one else," says Acts 4:12, "for there is no other name under heaven given to men by which we must be saved."

Our part is simple. The Bible says, "If you confess with your mouth, 'Jesus is Lord,' and believe in your heart that God raised him from the dead, you will be saved" (Romans 10:9).

You can do that now by simply and sincerely asking Him as best you know how to forgive your sins, be your Savior, and become the Lord of your life. You can bow your head and do that just as you are right now. Then follow it up by developing the habit of reading your Bible every day, learning to pray, attending a good church each week, and looking for ways to share your newfound faith with others.

Trusting Christ as your Savior is a decision that makes the angels sing!

Fallen Angels

The Origin of
Evil Angels

Is Satan an angelic being? Did the Devil, or Satan, start out as a created angel?

Yes, it seems Satan began as a top-ranked angel, perhaps an archangel, created by God at the beginning of time. There are two primary passages of Scripture about this—in Isaiah 14 and Ezekiel 28. Let's start with Isaiah 14, where the prophet Isaiah is expressing the love and compassion God had on ancient Israel and His intention to give the Jewish people a future of ultimate greatness. Verse 1 says, "The Lord will have compassion on Jacob; once again he will choose Israel and will settle them in their own land." Verse 4 talks about the defeat of Israel's enemies and how they will be laid low. At first, the passage seems to be referring to the human king of Babylon who would die and go to hell. But as we continue reading and get to verse 12, it appears Isaiah is actually talking about someone far more dangerous than a human enemy. The nature of the passage seems to suggest he is talking about the evil force behind the king of Babylon. Indeed, the title of "morning star" in verse 12 is, in the Hebrew language, the name "Lucifer."

Who is Lucifer?

Lucifer is a Hebrew word meaning "Morning Star" or "Day Star," and in Isaiah 14:12 it seems to be ascribed to the Devil. Lucifer is given many names in the Bible, including: the evil one (Matthew 5:37); the enemy (1 Peter 5:8); the accuser of our brothers and sisters (Revelation 12:10); Apollyon Abaddon and the destroyer (Revelation 9:11); murderer, liar, and the father of lies (John 8:44); the ruler of the kingdom of the air and the spirit now at work in those who are disobedient (Ephesians 2:2); the great dragon (Revelation 12:9); the tempter (Matthew 4:3); the thief (John 10:10); the enemy (Matthew 13:39); the ancient serpent (Revelation 12:9); the prince of this world (John 12:31); Beelzebul, the prince of demons (Matthew 12:24); and, of course, the Devil—a word that means accuser or slanderer.

How is Lucifer described in Isaiah 14?

Verse 12 says, "How you have fallen from heaven, morning star, son of the dawn! You have been cast down to the earth, you who once laid low the nations." While it is impossible to know exactly when this "fall" and "casting down" occurred, it would obviously have been after the creation (since angels are created beings; and at the conclusion of the creation process in Genesis 1:31 God pronounced His creation very good) and the appearance of the cunning serpent in the Garden of Eden in Genesis 3:1. In his original state, Lucifer was evidently a glorious angel, perhaps holding supreme authority in the angelic ranks. The words "morning star" and "son of the dawn" indicate splendor and authority. Yet he fell, rebelled, and was cast down to earth.

What caused Lucifer's rebellion?

According to Isaiah 14:13–14, Lucifer said to himself, "I will ascend to the heavens; I will raise my throne above the stars of God; I will sit enthroned on the mount of assembly, on the utmost heights. . . . I will ascend above the tops of the clouds; I will make myself like the Most High." Since angels (and all creation) are intended to glorify God, this is the origin of evil—a powerful angelic being who lusted in his heart for power and glory equaling or exceeding that of his Creator. Notice the prominence of the phrase *I will: I will ascend . . . I will raise . . . I will sit . . . I will make myself.* Compare that with what the Lord Jesus Christ prayed to His Father in the Garden of Gethsemane: "Not as I will, but as you will" (Matthew 26:39). It is evident that Lucifer's cry was the exact opposite of that of Christ. This was the ultimate Christ-unlikeness. This is the origin of pride and of all sin. Every sin is rooted in defiance and self-assertion. Pride is at the root of global evil and personal rebellion, and it all started when Lucifer avowed: "I will . . ."

What was God's reaction
to Lucifer's rebellion?

The next verse, Isaiah 14:15, pronounced Lucifer's doom: "But you are brought down to the realm of the dead, to the depths of the pit." This corresponds to many passages in the Bible that reassure us of Lucifer's ultimate defeat and banishment. The final biblical passage about this is Revelation 20:10: "And the devil, who deceived them, was thrown into the lake of burning sulfur, where the beast and the false prophet had been thrown. They will be tormented day and night for ever and ever."

When did the original rebellion happen?

Lucifer's rebellion occurred sometime between Genesis 1:31 and 3:1. In 1:31, God created the universe, saw all He had made, and pronounced it very good. This undoubtedly included the unseen world as well as the visible world, and this statement would seem to preclude the presence of sin and evil in the cosmos. Yet in 3:1, Lucifer appeared in the garden of Eden speaking diabolical words. So Lucifer's rebellion must have occurred sometime in the interval.

Turning to the parallel passage in Ezekiel 28, how is Lucifer described?

In this passage, the prophet Ezekiel was warning the city of Tyre and its king of coming judgment. Tyre was a great city to the north of Israel, and its king was a powerful force in ancient geopolitics. But in verse 28:11, the passage takes a strange turn and seems to describe the force of evil that lurks behind the king of Tyre. Many commentators believe the passage about the king of Tyre becomes a pronouncement against Lucifer, who was the one really in charge in the kingdom of Tyre. Verses 12 and 13 say of him: "You were the seal of perfection, full of wisdom and perfect in beauty. You were in Eden, the garden of God; every precious stone adorned you." Obviously the real king of Tyre was not in the garden of Eden before the creation of

Adam and Eve, nor was he perfect in wisdom and beauty. The one personality that fits that description is Lucifer.

Is Lucifer specifically referred to as an angel in Ezekiel 28?

Yes, as a cherub. Verses 14 and 15 say, "You were anointed as a guardian cherub, for so I ordained you. You were on the holy mount of God; you walked among the fiery stones. You were blameless in your ways from the day you were created." This tells us that Lucifer was a mighty angel, a guardian cherub, who had access to both heaven and earth. He traveled between the holy mount of God (heaven) and the garden of Eden (earth). He was arguably the most beautiful, powerful, wise, and exemplary of all God's creation to that point. He was, as Isaiah said, the son of the dawn, the bright and morning star. It's possible he was the leader of all the angels—God's five-star supreme commander of the armies of heaven. That would make him the highest of all the created order.

What ruined all this?

Ezekiel 28:15 is one of the most important verses in the Bible on the subject of evil. It says of Lucifer, "You were blameless in your ways from the day you were created till wickedness was found in you." As far as I can determine, this is the only verse in the Bible that tells us the origin of evil. We know God is holy, pure, perfect, and righteous in all His ways. His creation was unspoiled. His angelic hosts were sacred enough to dwell in His presence and do His bidding. But in one of them—a powerful, beautiful, resplendent cherub—evil occurred. It arose within him by spontaneous combustion. A slash of pride disturbed his heart, and in a flash he determined he wanted more—more power, more authority, more glory. Evil was found in him, and from him it spread to other angels and later to the human race itself.

What happened when God detected evil in Lucifer's heart?

The passage in Ezekiel 28 goes on to say, "You sinned. So I drove you in disgrace from the mount of God, and I expelled you, guardian cherub, from among the fiery stones. Your heart became proud on account of your beauty, and you corrupted your wisdom because of your splendor. So I threw you to the earth" (vv. 16–17). That's evidently where he met up with Eve. Having failed to get his way in heaven, he now set his nefarious sights on earth. Both Isaiah 14:12 and Ezekiel 28:17 speak specifically of Lucifer being cast down to our planet, where he shows up in Genesis 3 as the tempter.

Did any of the angelic hosts follow Lucifer in his rebellion against God?

Yes. We have a strong indication in Revelation 12 that a third of the angels followed Lucifer. Revelation 12:3 describes an enormous red dragon with seven heads and ten horns. This dragon is later identified as "that ancient serpent called the devil, or Satan, who leads the whole world astray" (v. 9). We're told that the dragon's tail "swept a third of the stars out of the sky and flung them to the earth" (v. 4). The Bible sometimes refers to angels as stars. Remember that the name *Lucifer* means "morning star." If the dragon swept a third of the stars from the sky, within the context of the chapter this would indicate he persuaded a third of all the heavenly host to follow him. A few verses later in this same passage, Revelation 12:9, we come across the phrase: "Satan . . . and his angels." It seems reasonably clear to me that the Bible teaches that a third of the angels fell from their positions of authority and became fallen angels, or demons, because of the sway of Lucifer's leadership and rebellion.

What other passages in the Bible speak of fallen angels?

Warning the church against false teachers, the apostle Peter said, "God did not spare angels when they sinned, but sent them to hell, putting them in chains of darkness" (2 Peter 2:4). The book of Jude has a similar warning: "And the angels who did not keep their positions of authority but abandoned their proper dwelling—these he has kept in darkness, bound with everlasting chains for judgment on the great Day" (Jude 6). Jesus was fully aware of this drama in the unseen world, for He predicted that when He comes again in judgment, He will say to the ungodly, "Depart from me, you who are cursed, into the eternal fire prepared for the devil and his angels" (Matthew 25:41). Hell seems to be the eternal zone where the devil and his angels will be incarcerated forever to keep them from disturbing the peace of heaven and of everlasting life.

Is Satan the opposite of God?

No. God is eternal; Satan had a beginning. God is limitless in His attributes; Satan, though powerful, is limited in all his properties. It's more accurate to think of Satan as the opposite of, say, the archangel Michael. Among other things, this means Satan cannot be everywhere at once. Like all angels, he can only be at one place at a time. Since there are innumerable demons, we have to assume there is a demonic network blanketing the globe, providing Satan with up-to-date intelligence about all that's going on. But he is not omnipresent (all present). That quality belongs to God alone. Nor is he omnipotent (all powerful) or omniscient (all knowing).

How does Satan attack God's children?

Satan wants to disrupt our lives in many ways. The book of Job opens with a description of Satanic attacks against the patriarch Job by causing the deaths of his children, the destruction of his wealth, and the deterioration of his health (Job 1–2). In Luke 22:31, Jesus told Peter and the other disciples, "Simon, Simon, Satan has asked to sift all of you as wheat." Later Peter wrote to his readers, saying, "Be alert and of sober mind. Your enemy the devil prowls around like a roaring lion looking for someone to devour. Resist him, standing firm in the faith" (1 Peter 5:8–9). The immediate reference here seems to indicate persecution. But Satan also intensifies the temptations we feel. First Chronicles 21:1 says, "Satan rose up against Israel and incited David to take a census of Israel"—something God had not willed. In Matthew 4, Satan even tried to tempt the Son of God and divert Him from His divine course. In Acts 5, Peter asked Ananias, "How is it that Satan has so filled your heart that you have lied to the Holy Spirit?" In biblical terms, the threat of Satan even extends to the most intimate areas of our marriage. Paul warned married couples of Corinth to enjoy frequent times of sexual intimacy "in order that Satan might not outwit us. For we are not unaware of his schemes" (2 Corinthians 2:11).

What else did the apostle Paul say about Satan?

In 1 Thessalonians 2:18, Paul told the Christians in the city of Thessalonica that he longed to visit them, but Satan had hindered him. This is an apparent reference to political and social conditions that prevented Paul from entering the city, but behind the problems the apostle saw the hand of the evil one. In 2 Corinthians 11:14–15, Paul warned the church in the city of Corinth to be discerning about the teachers they followed, "for Satan himself masquerades as an angel of light. It is not surprising, then, if his servants also masquerade as servants of righteousness." Paul also warned the Ephesians to be quick to forgive others. "Do not let the sun go down while you are still angry, and do not give the devil a foothold" (Ephesians 4:26–27). In light of these and other verses, we should take

Satan and his hosts very seriously. They have more to do with our disruptions, distresses, and temptations than we know.

Where are Satan's fallen angels right now?

Satan is on the loose. When a fugitive is running from the police, we say he or she is "in the wind." Well, we can rightly say Satan is in the wind. Ephesians 2:2 refers to Satan as "the ruler of the kingdom of the air, the spirit who is now at work in those who are disobedient." In terms of demons, many of them are also "in the wind," but some of the worst of them are currently being held in a sort of super-max prison that is called the "Pit" or the "Abyss." This seems to be where the most repulsive and dangerous demons are incarcerated for the time being. In Luke 8:31, a group of demons begged Jesus not to send them into the Abyss. In Revelation 9 and 11, we're told that during the Great Tribulation, vicious swarms of monster-demons will be released from the Abyss to torment the earth as part of the chaos and terror of the days immediately preceding the return of Christ. In Revelation 20, Satan himself will be imprisoned in the Abyss for a thousand years. Afterward, Satan and all his demons will be cast into hell, which was created by God as their eternal home. In summary, it appears for now that some of the demons are in the atmosphere and others are in the Abyss.

Are all the fallen angels currently in the Abyss?

No, legions of demons are encircling the earth now, seeking to disrupt the work of God's people and the mission of the church. Jesus frequently encountered demon-possessed people during His ministry (Matthew 9:32–33; 12:22–23; 17:14–18; Mark 5:1–20; 7:24–30; Luke 4:33–36), as did the apostles (Acts 5:16; 8:7; 16:16–18; 19:12–16). Additionally, both the Old and New Testaments contain stories of deceiving spirits, demons, and satanic influences at work in the world. The apostle Paul said in Ephesians 6:12, "For our struggle is not against flesh and blood, but against the rulers, against the authorities, against the powers of this dark world and against the spiritual forces of evil in the heavenly realms." This warfare is usually invisible to our eyes and inaudible to our ears, but it's real. There is constant warfare taking place in heavenly realms between angelic forces, good and evil. It spills over into our world. This is why Paul continued in Ephesians 6 to say, "Therefore put on the full armor of God" (v. 13). More about that later.

Demon Possession
and Powers

Does the presence of demons help explain the intensity of evil on earth?

Absolutely. Human beings are fallen, sinful creatures, but sometimes we detect periods and people of evil so intense there's no other explanation than demonic possession and influence. How else can we explain the horrors of child abuse, of genocide, of the beheading of innocent people, of the torture of families, of murder, rape, and the atrocities of war? How else can we explain the systematic attempts throughout history to exterminate Jews and Christians, as we see with Adolf Hitler and his cohorts?

Was Adolf Hitler
demon possessed?

In his book *Hitler's Cross*, Erwin W. Lutzer wrote, "Hitler was a thoroughly demonized being whose body was but the shell for the spirit that inhabited him." Lutzer points out that Hitler was mentored by a dedicated Satanist named Dietrich Echart, who "had been looking for a pupil, someone whom he could introduce to the spiritual forces." After Echart's death, Karl Haushofer assumed the job and took Hitler "into the deepest levels of occult transformation until he became a thoroughly demonized being." Hitler's personal magnetism, his ability to mesmerize audiences, and his drive to destroy the Jewish people can only be explained by his "personal acquaintance with satanic powers."[28] As we've seen, the passages about Lucifer in Isaiah 14 and Ezekiel 28 are addressed, in their immediate context, to earthly rulers. The implication is that much of the turmoil in the geopolitical world is prompted by satanic and demonic influences, and the level of pure evil exhibited by certain fanatical rulers and warlords can well be attributed to demonic power.

Why did Hitler hate
the Jews so much?

Satan despises the people of the Hebrews, for they represent God's original channel of redemption and salvation to the world, the nation through whom the Messiah would come. The nation of Israel is key to both the first and second coming of Christ. Satan repeatedly sought to disrupt our Lord's first coming by destroying the lineage of the Savior in the Old Testament. Hence we have the stories of Cain in the book of Genesis, Pharaoh in the book of Exodus, Haman in the book of Esther, and Antiochus IV in the period between the Old and New Testaments. The Gospels open with King Herod slaying the babies of Bethlehem, seeking to eradicate the Savior. Nonetheless, Jesus lived, died, and rose from the grave. Now in these last days the nation of Israel has been reborn and is once again at the heart of prophecies regarding the Second Coming. Knowing this, Satan has repeatedly tried for the last two thousand years to destroy the Jewish people. He is desperate to disrupt the Second Coming, which, like the first coming, cannot take place apart from the fulfillment of prophecies about the nation of Israel. This is Satan's "final solution." The Holocaust was pure, demonized, genocidal evil. But Hitler was only a foreshadowing of a coming man of lawlessness called the Antichrist; not even the Holocaust can compare to Satan's future attempt to destroy Israel in coming days during the Great Tribulation. Current events are hurtling us toward that day like a cannonball from a catapult.

The Bible indicates people can be possessed by demons, but can an individual be possessed by the Devil himself?

Satan possession seems to be more rare than demon possession. Without being dogmatic, it seems to me there are three cases of satanic possession in the Bible. The first is the serpent in the garden of Eden. We get the impression that Satan commandeered and possessed an animal, through whom he spoke to Eve. The second case is Judas Iscariot, the man who betrayed Christ. John 13:27 says, "As soon as Judas took the bread, Satan entered into him." The third case seems to be the aforementioned Antichrist, who is repeatedly pictured in the Bible as possessing satanic powers, which he will use to terrorize the earth in the last days.

What are the characteristics of demon possession or demonic influence?

In Mark 5 and Luke 8, Jesus met a man possessed by multiple demons. This man had an obsession with death and "lived in the tombs" (Mark 5:2). He had bursts of violent strength and ungovernable impulses (vv. 3–4). He was self-destructive (v. 5:5). He indulged in nudity (Luke 8:27). He had antisocial behaviors (v. 29). In his book, *Angels: Elect and Evil*, C. Fred Dickason wrote, "Since their rebellion with Satan, demons are morally and spiritually unclean. Their total capacities as persons were perverted. . . . Their nature and realm of operation is moral darkness. . . . They are termed 'unclean spirits' or 'evil spirits.' . . . Demons' immorality is often manifest in the sensuousness of those they control or influence."[29]

What happened to Legion and his demons in the Gospels?

Jesus asked the man his name, and he replied, "Legion," for he was possessed with many demons. These evil spirits then began begging Jesus not to send them to the Abyss (that supernatural, super-max prison I described earlier). Interestingly, Jesus agreed to their request. Luke 8:32–33 says, "A large herd of pigs was feeding there on the hillside. The demons begged Jesus to let them go into the pigs, and he gave them permission. When the demons came out of the man, they went into the pigs, and the herd rushed down the steep bank into the lake and was drowned."

What happened to the demons after the pigs drowned isn't told, but notice that the demons wrought self-destructive influence over both the man and the swine. Satan wants to destroy us, but he finds fiendish pleasure when he can get us to destroy ourselves. Those under demonic influence are both destructive and self-destructive. In his book *Systematic Theology*, Wayne Grudem wrote, "The tactics of Satan and his demons are to use lies (John 8:44), deception (Revelation 12:9), murder (Psalm 106:37; John 8:44), and every other kind of destructive activity to attempt to cause people to turn away from God and destroy themselves."[30]

Are there other examples of animals being possessed by demons?

Not in Scripture, unless you consider the serpent in Genesis 3 or the hideous creatures in the book of Revelation. But there are some interesting stories from missionary history. For example, one day as missionary Dick Hillis (1913–2005) preached in a Chinese village, his sermon was interrupted by a piercing cry. Everyone rushed toward the scream, and Dick's coworker, Mr. Kong, whispered that an evil spirit had seized a man. "That is heathen superstition," said Dick, who had not previously encountered demon possession.

A woman pushed through the crowd toward them. "I beg you, help me!" she cried. "An evil spirit has again possessed the father of my children and is trying to kill him."

Stepping over a filthy old dog lying in the doorway, Mr. Kong faced the madman. The room was charged with a sense of evil. Mr. Kong asked Dick to begin singing the hymn "There Is Power in the Blood." With great hesitation, Dick began to sing, "Would you be free from your burden of sin . . ."

"Now," continued Mr. Kong, "in the name of Jesus we will command the evil spirit to leave this man." Mr. Kong began praying fervently. Suddenly, the old dog in the doorway vaulted into the air, screeching, yelping, whirling in circles, snapping wildly at his tail. Mr. Kong continued praying, and the dog abruptly dropped over dead. Instantly Dick remembered Luke 8 and the demons of the Gadarenes who had invisibly flown into the herd of swine. As Mr. Kong finished praying, Farmer Ho seemed quiet and relaxed, and soon he was strong enough to burn his idols. At his baptism shortly afterward, he testified, "I was possessed by an evil spirit who boasted he had already killed five people and was going to kill me. But God sent Mr. Kong at just the right moment, and in Jesus I am free."[31]

Do demonic powers operate on a geopolitical level as well as a personal level?

Yes. We see examples of both in the Bible. There is a spiritual grid around the world where an intense battle is raging unseen by human eyes. On several occasions in the Old Testament, kings and other leaders were tricked into making disastrous decisions because of "lying spirits" who deceived them (Judges 9:23; 1 Kings 22:22; 1 Chronicles 21:1; 2 Chronicles 18:18–22). On an individual level, according to Ephesians 6:16, Satan is an archer who shoots flaming arrows our way, which we must deflect with the shield of faith. Along the way, some people become so ensnared by demonic power they are said to be demon possessed, or, more accurately, to have demons.

I think it's worth noting that God is not the author of evil, and He does not tempt us toward evil (James 1:13). He does permit Satan and the demonic powers to tempt us. There is, therefore, a sense in which God is in control of all things, even when He allows things to happen that don't correspond to His holiness. As an example, 1 Chronicles 21:1 says, "Satan rose up against Israel and incited David to take a census." But 2 Samuel 24:1 refers to the same incident, saying, "The anger of the LORD burned against Israel, and he incited David against them, saying, 'Go and take a census . . .'" Satan was the direct agent responsible for the evil, but God permitted it. In the same way, 2 Thessalonians 2:11 says, relating to Satan's work, "For this reason God sends them a powerful delusion so that they will believe the lie." The active agent of evil is Satan, but God allows the activity to occur for now. In terms of geopolitical intrigues, the demonic powers are inciting evil, but it will all work toward God's preordained ends.

Can demonic powers affect our prayers?

As incredible as it sounds, Satan and his fallen forces are so powerful they may even attempt to interrupt the answers God decrees to our prayers. As we saw earlier in the book, one of the most astonishing passages in the Bible about fallen angels and spiritual warfare is Daniel 10. In this passage, Daniel earnestly prayed for insight regarding a prophecy he had received. He fasted and prayed for three weeks. Finally an angel flew into his presence and explained, "Do not be afraid, Daniel. Since the first day that you set your mind to gain understanding and to humble yourself before your God, your words were heard, and I have come in response to them. But the prince of the Persian kingdom resisted me twenty-one days. Then Michael, one of the chief princes, came to help me, because I was detained there with the king of Persia. Now I have come to explain to you what will happen to your people in the future, for the vision concerns a time yet to come."

It seems from the passage that when Daniel prayed and asked for information, the Lord immediately dispatched an angel with the requested data. But the messenger was intercepted. He was hindered and held back by someone called the prince of the Persian kingdom. This foe evidently wasn't a human being, for the delay and conflict took place in the passageway between earth and heaven. Apparently a demon assigned to the Persian kingdom opposed the angel who was bringing Daniel's answer to prayer, and the stalemate lasted three weeks. The archangel Michael joined the battle, and his superior authority finally won the day and allowed the divine messenger to deliver God's answer to Daniel.

While this passage is mysterious, it gives us a glimpse into the spiritual warfare constantly occurring between heaven and earth and between good angels and fallen ones. Sometimes—though we may not realize it—we're caught in the middle. The superior power, however, resides with the good angels, and the ultimate power belongs to Him who said, "All authority in heaven and on earth has been given to me" (Matthew 28:18).

Can Christians be demon possessed?

Most Bible scholars do not believe a Christian can be demon possessed because the Bible teaches that when we receive Christ as our Lord and Savior, His blood covers us and forgives us, and the Holy Spirit comes to live within us. "Do you not know that your bodies are temples of the Holy Spirit, who is in you, whom you have received from God," says 1 Corinthians 6:19. Since demons are incompatible with the blood of Christ and the indwelling of the Holy Spirit, it would seem that Satan or his demons couldn't possess Christians. But there's a caveat. Technically, the term "possessed" isn't the best or most accurate phrase for what happens when a demon enters a person, even though that designation appears in many English translations of the New Testament and I'm using it in this book. The original Greek versions simply spoke of people *having* demons. There's no doubt that even Christians can be targeted by demonic forces, hence the cautions in the New Testament about resisting the devil, being aware of his schemes, and suiting ourselves with the armor of the Spirit. As Christians, we must always stay on guard.

How did the apostle Paul respond to demon possession?

In Acts 16, the apostle Paul and his coworker Silas were seeking to establish a church in the Macedonian city of Philippi, but they were harassed by a demon-possessed girl who is described in Acts 16:16 as "a female slave who had a spirit by which she predicted the future. She earned a great deal of money for her owners by fortune-telling." This woman followed the evangelists around as though mesmerized by them, and verse 18 says, "Paul become so annoyed that he turned around and said to the spirit, 'In the name of Jesus Christ I command you to come out of her!' At that moment the spirit left her." Because the owners realized their scheme of making money was gone, they seized Paul and Silas and had the two Christians flogged and imprisoned.

Can demons and those with demons predict the future?

Remember that Satan is not the opposite of God. The devil is not omniscient and cannot know the future as God does. Yet he does try to imitate God's attributes and powers. He certainly has insights into the direction the future is taking, and he also undoubtedly knows what he himself is planning to do. Demons also know the Scriptures and are students of prophecy. They are evidently able to make calculated and accurate "guesses" about the future, and we should assume that someone purporting to tell our future may be under demonic influence.

Is it okay to read horoscopes, consult Ouija boards and tarot cards, and sometimes visit fortune-tellers?

It is never wise to do so. In Deuteronomy 18:9–11, Moses told the Israelites, "When you enter the land the LORD your God is giving you, do not learn to imitate the detestable ways of the nations there. Let no one be found among you who sacrifices their son or daughter in the fire, who practices divination or sorcery, interprets omens, engages in witchcraft, or casts spells, or who is a medium or spiritist or who consults the dead."

What should our attitude be toward the occult—witchcraft, fortune-telling, astrology, necromancy, and the like?

Isaiah 8:19–20 has a succinct answer: "When someone tells you to consult mediums and spiritists, who whisper and mutter, should not a people inquire of their God? Why consult the dead on behalf of the living? Consult God's instruction." Everything we need to know about the future is revealed to us in God's Word. The Bible is packed with predictive prophecy, and as it relates to our own daily lives, we have constant promises of God's guidance. The children of the Lord should never consult Satan or any satanic source for direction in life. In Leviticus 20:6–7, God said, "I will set my face against anyone who turns to mediums and spiritists to prostitute themselves by following them, and I will cut them off from their people. Consecrate yourselves to be holy, because I am the LORD your God."

Should we be afraid of demons?

No, and we should guard against obsessing about them. Many people struggle with issues in their lives that are spiritual, emotional, chemical, medical, or environmental. While it's true that Satan and his forces can complicate our lives, we should be slow to attribute too many problems to direct demon possession or oppression.

As Jesus traveled throughout Galilee, He occasionally encountered someone who was demon possessed, but most of the people He met were simply suffering from temptation, sin, fatigue, illness, rejection, need, lack of direction, or lostness. Sometimes He cast out demons, but more frequently He preached the gospel, taught the Scriptures, nurtured His followers, debated His enemies, and cared for the needy.

Jesus was aware of Satan's influence over their lives, but He did not always identify this influence as possession. In John 8:44, He told His opponents, "You belong to your father, the devil, and you want to carry out your father's desires. He was a murderer from the beginning, not holding to the truth, for there is no truth in him. When he lies, he speaks his native language, for he is a liar and the father of lies." These are certainly interesting insights about Satan, and Jesus clearly understood these enemies were members of Satan's family rather than members of God's family, but He stopped short of calling them demon possessed or seeking to cast demons out of them. I believe demon possession may be somewhat rare, but demonic influence is pervasive in our world.

What did the great reformer Martin Luther have to say about the Devil?

There are several stories of Luther's conflicts with the devil. One of my favorite quotes by Martin Luther was spoken when he was ordered to travel to the German city of Worms to defend himself before the emperor. His friends advised him to run in the other direction. Luther famously replied, "I am lawfully called to appear in that city, and thither I will go in the name of the Lord, though as many devils as there are tiles on the houses were there combined against me."[32] Luther expressed the same thought in his renowned hymn, "A Mighty Fortress Is Our God":

And though this world, with devils filled,
    should threaten to undo us,
We will not fear, for God hath willed His truth
    to triumph through us.

How should we respond when Satan and his demonic forces threaten to undo us?

Everything depends on knowing Jesus Christ as Savior. There's more power in one drop of the shed blood of Christ than in all the demonic forces combined. Acts 20:28 refers to Christians as "the church of God, which he bought with his own blood." Romans 5:9 says, "We have now been justified by his blood." Ephesians 1:7 says, "We have redemption through his blood." Ephesians 2:13 adds, we "have been brought near by the blood of Christ." Hebrews 9:14 says, "How much more, then, will the blood of Christ . . . cleanse our consciences from acts that lead to death, so that we may serve the living God." According to Hebrews 10:19, "we have confidence to enter the Most Holy Place by the blood of Jesus." Hebrews 13:12 says that Christ has made us holy "through his own blood." And Revelation 12:11 says about those martyred for Christ during the Great Tribulation: "They triumphed over him by the blood of the Lamb and by the word of their testimony; they did not love their lives so much as to shrink from death."

Has our victory over Satan's forces of evil already been won by Christ?

Affirmative. Hebrews 2:14–15 says of Christ, "Since the children have flesh and blood, he too shared in their humanity so that by his death he might break the power of him who holds the power of death—that is, the devil—and free those who all their lives were held in slavery by their fear of death." In other words, Jesus is God the Son, the second person of the Trinity, who became a human being in order to die and rise again. Taking Satan's own weapon—death—He defeated Satan. It's reminiscent of when the shepherd boy David fought Goliath. Having knocked the giant over with a stone from his slingshot, David took the giant's own sword and decapitated him. Using the devil's own weapon of death, Jesus defeated him.

When our Lord died on the cross, Satan surely thought he had emerged as the victor in his epic struggle against God, but three days later the tables were turned. Jesus is victor! As Christians, we're included in Christ's resurrection victory over the forces of evil. Colossians 2:13–15 says:

> God made you alive with Christ. He forgave us all our sins, having canceled the charge of our legal indebtedness, which stood against us and condemned us; he has taken it away, nailing it to the cross. And having disarmed the powers and authorities, he made a public spectacle of them, triumphing over them by the cross.

How do I appropriate the blood of Christ for my own forgiveness and protection?

That happens when we confess our sins and acknowledge Jesus Christ as our crucified and resurrected Savior and Lord. The Bible says, "It was not with perishable things such as silver or gold that you were redeemed from the empty way of life handed down to you from your ancestors, but with the precious blood of Christ, a lamb without blemish or defect. He was chosen before the creation of the world, but was revealed in these last times for your sake. Through him you believe in God, who raised him from the dead and glorified him, and so your faith and hope are in God" (1 Peter 1:18–21). Making a personal commitment to turn to Christ in repentance and faith is the greatest and safest decision of our lives.

Having become a Christian, am I now immune to Satan's temptations?

No. Satan has been defeated but he's like a decapitated snake that can still bite. Though his power was broken at Calvary, his ultimate doom doesn't occur until the end of world history (Revelation 20:7–10). Until then, we're told to "put on the whole armor of God, so that you can take your stand against the devil's schemes." We must always be on guard, constantly remembering the promise of Romans 16:20: "The God of peace will soon crush Satan under your feet. The grace of the Lord Jesus be with you."

As a Christian, how do I respond to satanic temptations and demonic attacks?

We grow stronger against Satan as we grow stronger in Christ, so we have an obligation to Christian maturity. Paul told Timothy to choose seasoned people as church overseers. The church leader, Paul said, must "have a good reputation with outsiders, so that he will not fall into disgrace and into the devil's trap" (1 Timothy 3:7). We must keep our habits pure and holy. Pride, anger, bitterness, and sexual temptations are the playground of the devil (1 Corinthians 7:5; Ephesians 4:27; 1 Timothy 3:6; 2 Timothy 2:26).

An excellent passage about this is 2 Corinthians 2:10–11, having to do with keeping our hearts in a loving mood toward others. Paul said, "Anyone you forgive, I also forgive. And what I have forgiven—if there was anything to forgive—I have forgiven in the sight of Christ for your sake, in order that Satan might not outwit us. For we are not unaware of his schemes."

The mark of true spirituality is keeping our hearts and habits Christlike as we grow up into Christ in all things. We should be sensitive to sin, quick to confess anything that hinders our fellowship with God, and eager to further develop our daily walk with Christ through prayer, Bible study, faith, and obedience.

Are there some particular verses I should memorize on this subject?

Yes, James and Peter give us two succinct statements worth learning. James 4:7–8 says, "Submit yourselves, then, to God. Resist the devil, and he will flee from you. Come near to God and he will come near to you." Peter makes the same point with a vivid analogy: "Be alert and of sober mind. Your enemy the devil prowls around like a roaring lion looking for someone to devour. Resist him, standing firm in the faith" (1 Peter 5:8–9).

How do we resist the Devil?

To resist the Devil, we need a good defense. We need the whole armor of the Holy Spirit to protect us. Ephesians 6:10–16 tells us:

> Be strong in the Lord and in his mighty power, which we do when we put on "the full armor of God, so that you can take your stand against the devil's schemes. For our struggle is not against flesh and blood, but against the rulers, against the authorities, against the powers of this dark world and against the spiritual forces of evil in the heavenly realms. Therefore put on the full armor of God, so that when the day of evil comes, you may be able to stand your ground, and after you have done everything, to stand."

The apostle Paul proceeds to inventory the various pieces of the Christian's armor:

- the belt of truth
- the breastplate of righteousness
- feet fitted with the readiness that comes from the gospel of peace
- the shield of faith, with which you can extinguish all the flaming arrows of the evil one
- the helmet of salvation
- the sword of the Spirit, which is the Word of God

How is the Word of God like a sword we can use against Satan?

All the other pieces of armor mentioned in Ephesians 6 are defensive, but the last one brings us to a second great strategy against Satan. We can take the offense. The Bible refers to itself as being "sharper than any doubled-edged sword" (Hebrews 4:12). When we quote Scripture, the devil has no answer to give us. He can argue with us, but the Bible is the supreme written code of the universe. This was how Christ Himself resisted the devil on the mount of temptation in Matthew 4:1–11. At each of the three temptations, Jesus quoted scriptures He had evidently memorized. We should do the same. Most of us know our points of vulnerability. If you're short-tempered, learn some critical Bible verses about anger, patience, and long-suffering. If you have addictive tendencies, search out those scriptures that speak of breaking free from slavery and bondage. If you have bitter feelings toward someone, there are lots of verses dealing with forgiveness and love. Everyone has a different set of battles, but there are verses covering every sphere of human temptation and struggle. Find the ones that fit your situation. Learn them. Memorize some of them. Post them. Quote them. Remember Psalm 119:11: "I have hidden your word in my heart that I might not sin against you."

Can I rebuke the Devil?

Theologian Wayne Grudem avows, "Jesus gives all believers authority to rebuke demons and command them to leave."[33] In both the Gospels and the book of Acts, Jesus empowered His followers to resist and rebuke satanic spirits. The apostle John told the Christians of his day, "Every spirit that does not acknowledge Jesus is not from God. This is the spirit of the antichrist, which you have heard is coming and even now is already in the world. You, dear children, are from God and have overcome them, because the one who is in you is greater than the one who is in the world" (1 John 4:3–4).

Many of our problems in life may not represent a direct satanic attack, but sometimes they do, as we see in the opening chapters of the book of Job. In times of intense temptation or oppression, God's children can always say in Jesus' name, as

Jesus Himself did: "Away from me, Satan! For it is written . . ." and then quote an appropriate verse of Scripture (Matthew 4:10).

Is it possible to become too obsessed over Satan?

Yes, we should never brood over demonism or let our thoughts be absorbed with satanic obsessions. The Holocaust survivor and evangelist Corrie ten Boom wrote, "We must be careful not to advertise the devil by talking too much about him and his devices."[34] Although the apostle Paul blamed the devil for many of the problems he encountered in his ministry, it's also true that Paul, in reality, focused on Christ. He said in 1 Corinthians 14:20, "In regard to evil be infants." I've written previously in *The Red Sea Rules,* "We always make a mistake when we acknowledge the Lord and keep our eyes on Satan. Far better to acknowledge the devil while keeping our eyes on Christ. . . . In the Pauline letters, the word *Jesus* occurs in 219 verses, the word *Lord* in 272 verses, and the word *Christ* in 389 verses. *Satan,* on the other hand, occurs in only 10 verses, and the word *devil* in only 6."[35]

Can fallen angels
read our minds?

There's no evidence that Satan or his fallen angels can read our minds. They are not omniscient like God, but, like the good angels, they are creatures with superior intellects and powers. They are students of human behavior and can often anticipate and exploit our weaknesses. Paradoxically, they are also students of Scripture. For them, studying the Bible is like reading the enemy's game plan. They also believe in God, but not with obedience. James 2:19 says, "You believe that there is one God. Good! Even the demons believe that—and shudder."

Satan and Fallen Angels in the Last Days

What role do Satan and the fallen angels play in the last days?

The book of Revelation is filled with dramatic information about the role of Satan and the satanic hosts, who will terrorize the world during the Great Tribulation. Revelation 9 describes the hordes of demons who will be unleashed on the earth:

> I saw a star that had fallen from the sky to the earth. The star was given the key to the shaft of the Abyss. When he opened the Abyss, smoke rose from it like the smoke from a gigantic furnace. The sun and sky were darkened by the smoke from the Abyss. And out of the smoke locusts came down on the earth and were given power like scorpions of the earth. (vv. 1–3)

These "scorpions" have a king over them, who is called the "angel of the Abyss, whose name in Hebrew is Abaddon and in Greek is Apollyon (that is, the Destroyer)" (v. 11). These scorpions are a particularly vicious variety of demons, and they serve their king, the Destroyer, or the Devil. These are some of the worst of the worst. While they are currently imprisoned in the super-max prison of the Abyss, they will be unleashed on the earth during the Tribulation.

What happens to fallen angels during the Tribulation?

Revelation 9:14–16 then describes more hordes of increasingly vicious demons who will escape from the Abyss: "And the four [evil] angels who had been kept ready for this very hour and day and month and year were released to kill a third of mankind. The number of the mounted troops was twice ten thousand times ten thousand. I heard their number."

The passage provides a terrifying description of these twisted, grotesque, evil spirits. Verse 19, for example, says: "Their tails were like snakes, having heads with which they inflict injury."

Yet despite the terror and destruction caused by these demonic armies, the surviving humans in those days remained defiant against God. "The rest of mankind who were not killed by these plagues still did not repent of the work of their hands; they did not stop worshiping demons" (v. 20).

Are there yet more demons in the Abyss who will escape or be released during the Tribulation?

Sadly, yes. A subsequent passage, Revelation 16:12–16, says:

> The sixth angel poured out his bowl on the great river Euphrates, and its water was dried up to prepare the way for the kings of the East. Then I saw three impure spirits that looked like frogs; they came out of the mouth of the dragon, out of the mouth of the beast and out of the mouth of the false prophet. They are demonic spirits that perform signs, and they go out to the kings of the whole world and gather them for the battle on the great day of God Almighty. . . . Then they gathered the kings together to the place that in Hebrew is called Armageddon.

Just as demonic powers influenced geopolitical events in Old Testament days, so it will be in the last days. The human armies and nations that survive the turmoil of the Great Tribulation will be directed by demonic forces to muster in the great valley of Armageddon for a final assault on Jerusalem. Their goal is the same one Satan has harbored in his heart from the day he prompted Cain to kill Abel—to destroy the Jewish people and the lineage of redemption and to prevent the coming of Christ.

Who will provide the face of leadership on the earth during the Great Tribulation?

That will be the Antichrist. He will be a human being, but he will be possessed and empowered by demons, or more likely by Satan himself. The Bible repeatedly talks about this man's extraordinary charisma, mesmerizing power, remarkable leadership, vaulting pride, blasphemous words, and miraculous power. But his authority is derived from Satan. Revelation 13 compares Satan to a dragon and the Antichrist to a beast. "The whole world was filled with wonder and followed the beast. People worshiped the dragon because he had given authority to the beast, and they also worshiped the beast" (vv. 3–4). Likewise, 2 Thessalonians 2:9 says of the Antichrist: "The coming of the lawless one will be in accordance with how Satan works. He will use all sorts of displays of power through signs and wonders that serve the lie." The Antichrist will be Satan's ultimate human agent.

What will be the final result of the Antichrist?

At the very moment of the outbreak of Armageddon, Jesus will return and the battle will be won almost before it's even fought. The Bible says, "And then the lawless one [the Antichrist] will be revealed, whom the Lord Jesus will overthrow with the breath of his mouth and destroy by the splendor of his coming" (2 Thessalonians 2:8). Zechariah 14 says, "I will gather all the nations to Jerusalem to fight against it. . . . Then the Lord will go out and fight against those nations, as he fights on a day of battle. On that day his feet will stand on the Mount of Olives. . . . On that day living water will flow. . . . The Lord will be king over the whole earth" (vv. 2, 3, 4, 8, 9). Jesus put it like this: "Then will appear the sign of the Son of Man in heaven. And then all the peoples of the earth will mourn when they see the Son of Man coming in the clouds of heaven, with power and great glory" (Matthew 24:30). The apostle Paul said, "This will happen when the Lord Jesus is revealed from heaven in blazing fire with his powerful angels. He will punish those who do not know God" (2 Thessalonians 1:7–8). The apostle John describes the second coming of Christ like this in Revelation 19:11–20:

> I saw heaven standing open and there before me was a white horse, whose rider is called Faithful and True. With justice he judges and wages war. His eyes are like blazing fire, and on his head are many crowns. . . . Then I saw the beast and the kings of the earth and their armies gathered together to wage war against the rider on the horse and his army. But the beast was captured, and with it the false prophet who had performed the signs on its behalf.

What then will happen to Satan and all the fallen angels upon Christ's return?

In due time, all are condemned to hell for eternity, never again to trouble heaven or earth. Revelation 20:10 says, "The devil . . . was thrown into the lake of burning sulfur, where the beast and the false prophet had been thrown. They will be tormented day and night for ever and ever." Hell is the place prepared for the devil and his angels (Matthew 25:41).

It's worth noting that Satan is not in the first two chapters of the Bible, and he is not in the last two. In the first two chapters he has not yet shown up in the human story; and in the last two chapters he's imprisoned in hell and unable to ever again disturb us.

What is the central message about fallen angels in the book of Revelation?

As we've seen from earlier passages in Isaiah and Ezekiel and in the temptation of Christ in Matthew 4, Satan's great objective is to be like God. Since he cannot literally and actually be God, he tries to counterfeit the Godhead. Just as there are three persons in the Godhead—Father, Son, and Holy Spirit—Satan will form a diabolical trinity made up of himself, the Antichrist, and the false prophet in the days described in the book of Revelation (Revelation 13; 16:13; 19:20). The points of similarity are a remarkable study, as though Satan were trying to replicate in a diabolical, twisted way everything that represents who God is and what God does. Dr. J. Oswald Sanders, missionary statesman (1902–1992), listed the points of similarity he had observed in his years of Bible study and overseas ministry:

- Satan has his own trinity: the devil, the beast, and the false prophet (Revelation 16:13).
- He has his own church, "a synagogue of Satan" (Revelation 2:9).
- He has his own ministers, "ministers of Satan" (2 Corinthians 11:4–5).
- He has formulated his own system of theology, "doctrines of demons" (1 Timothy 4:1).
- He has established his own sacrificial system; "The Gentiles . . . sacrifice to demons" (1 Corinthians 10:20).
- He has his own communion service, "the cup of demons . . . and the table of demons" (1 Corinthians 10:21).
- His ministers proclaim his own gospel, "a gospel contrary to that which we have preached to you" (Galatians 1:7–8).
- He has his own throne (Revelation 13:2) and his own worshipers (Revelation 13:4).[36]

What is the summarization of all this?

Revelation 6–18 provides insights into the final years of world history, which will be a time of the Great Tribulation, in which the "evil trinity" will seize control of world government and seek to destroy the nation of Israel. Millions of vicious demons will escape up the smoking shaft of the Abyss and torment the world. A convergence of events will intersect at Armageddon, and then, like a thief in the night, Jesus will suddenly return. Satan and his axis of evil will be defeated and eternally banished. No longer will there be any curse. God's blood-bought children will live with Him in His eternal home, along with the holy angels who will be our friends and fellow servants. It's said of those of us who know Jesus: "They will see His face, and His name will be on their foreheads. There will be no more night. . . . And they will reign for ever and ever" (Revelation 22:4–5).

Any more advice about angels and demons?

Yes. Sing! Learn the great hymns of the faith as well as newer songs of praise, and fill your heart and home with godly music. Missionary hero Amy Carmichael (1867–1951) of Dohnavur, India, once wrote to a friend, saying, "I wonder if you feel as I do about the heavenliness of song. I believe truly that Satan cannot endure it, and so slips out of the room—more or less!—when there is true song."[37]

In *Then Sings My Soul: Book 3*, I relate a story told to me by Cliff Barrows, the longtime music director for the Billy Graham crusades. Cliff said his father, Charles Tilson Barrows, was very involved in the Bible distribution ministry of the Gideons. On one occasion he traveled to Rangoon. The area was under an oppressive government, and Gideon Bibles had been removed from the hotel rooms. While there, Mr. Barrows attended a meeting of the local Gideons who were trying to get Bibles back into the hotels. During the meeting two men were singing hymns in one end of the room, and the singing was disruptive. Barrows had trouble following the discussions because the two hymn-singers were going at it a few yards away. Finally he asked, "Why are those men singing while we're trying to have this meeting?"

The local Gideon replied, "Because this room is bugged, and the singing confuses the enemy who is trying to listen to us."

Glancing over to me, Cliff said, "There's a spiritual lesson in that. When we sing, it confuses the enemy and allows the Lord's work to proceed."[38]

In the story of King Jehoshaphat in 2 Chronicles 20, the kingdom of Judah was about to be invaded by an overwhelming mass of enemy forces. The king called the people to prayer, and then he devised the most unusual strategy in military history. Verses 21–22 say:

Jehoshaphat appointed men to sing to the Lord and to praise him for the splendor of his holiness as they went out at the head of the army, saying: 'Give thanks to the Lord, for his love endures forever.' As they began to sing and praise, the LORD set ambushes against the [enemy].

Perhaps we should develop a similar strategy. The forces of evil hate it when they hear us singing songs about the blood of Christ, the resurrection of our Lord, and the lordship of the coming King. Let's confuse the enemy, sing about the power of Jesus' name, and give thanks to the Lord, for His love endures forever.

What in the Bible is most surprising about good and evil angels?

I'm amazed at how much information God has revealed to us in Scripture. When the Creator formed the cosmos, He made a visible realm and an invisible one. Colossians 1:16 says, referring to Christ, "For in Him all things were created: things in heaven and on earth, visible and invisible, whether thrones or powers or rulers or authorities; all things have been created through him and for him." At the dawning of eternity, God will merge these two dimensions—the physical and the spiritual—into a unified whole. According to Ephesians 1:10, God has made known to us His will, which He purposed in Christ, "to be put into effect when the times reach their fulfillment—to bring unity to all things in heaven and on earth under Christ."

Until then we're living in a divided and dual universe—a visible sphere and an invisible one. And much of the action affecting our lives and our world is occurring in the invisible realm. We would have known little or nothing about this, except for one thing: God saw fit to give His children a Book explaining it in considerable detail. In the Bible, we have a progressive unfolding description of the cosmic battle occurring around us. We're told the origin of evil and how God confronted it at Calvary. We're told the finality of evil and how God's children will triumph in the end. We're told of angels and demons, of principalities and powers, of death and resurrection, of time and eternity.

From the first chapters of Genesis to the final chapters of Revelation, the Bible gives us answers to questions about angels—wonderful answers, satisfying answers, remarkable answers. And the more we study this subject in Scripture, the more we want to sing with all our hearts:

> All hail the power of Jesus' name!
> Let angels prostrate fall;
> Bring forth the royal diadem,
> And crown Him Lord of all.

Conclusion

Just as I was finishing this book, I heard from James Martin—the brother of a friend of mine—who served in the US Air Force during an overseas conflict. He and his men were assigned a dangerous patch of ground to patrol night after night. There were seven men in his squad, and James assigned three men to each side of the territory while he took the middle section. "We identified each other using clickers much like a childhood cricket toy I once had," he said. "This kept us from having to talk and use passwords."

One night when the moon was bright and the enemy could see them more clearly, James was patrolling with a sense of apprehension. Suddenly a voice behind him spoke distinctly and with urgency: "Stop! Take one step back!" James complied immediately. He instantly felt a tug at his left sleeve and heard the crack of gunfire. Falling to the ground, he started firing his M-16 in the direction of the shots. His two groups converged on his position from opposite directions and were able to drive back the enemy from the perimeter.

"When I got back to the barracks," James told me, "there was a bullet hole through my left sleeve. The angle of the hole was about thirty to forty-five degrees, and I measured the distance from the hole to the center of the shirt. I then realized that voice saved my life. Had I not complied, the bullet would have struck the center of my chest."

James questioned his men, but none of them had been near him and none had spoken to him. Though time has passed, James is still convinced the voice he heard was angelic. "I believe in angels," he told me. "I always have. I don't think one can believe in good angels without believing in evil ones. I know the devil is always around, but I'm comforted by knowing the Lord sends His angels to protect us and watch over us too."*

As we've seen, Hebrews 1:14 says, "Are not all

_____

* Because this was a classified mission, the name of the individual has been changed and the details of when and where this happened have been omitted. Otherwise I have relayed the account exactly as told me.

angels ministering spirits sent to serve those who will inherit salvation?" That means God provides angelic oversight to His children, to those who have been redeemed and saved by the power of the death and resurrection of Jesus Christ. The Bible says, "Christ died for our sins according to the Scriptures. . . . He was buried. . . . He was raised on the third day" (1 Corinthians 15:3–4).

The most important message in this book isn't about angels; the most important message is about the Lord Jesus Christ. He can do far more for us than angels can. He died for us and rose again; no angel could do that. He can give us eternal life; no angel can do that. He loves us with an everlasting love, and He calls us to be His followers forever. It's not angels we worship and serve, but Christ, who must have supremacy in all things (Colossians 1:18).

Angels represent a fascinating biblical subject, but only Jesus is Lord of heaven and earth. Give Him your heart and pledge your loyalty to Him. Turn to Him in repentance and faith and let Him be Lord of every area of your life. Become His faithful follower and heir of His blessings. Let's join the angels who encircle His throne and say with them:

"Worthy is the Lamb, who was slain, to receive power and wealth and wisdom and strength and honor and glory and praise! . . . To him who sits on the throne and to the Lamb be praise and honor and glory and power, forever and ever . . . Amen!" (Revelation 5:12–14).

Endnotes

1. Richard Hendrix in an interview with the author. Used with permission.
2. *The Table Talk of Martin Luther*, translated by William Hazlitt (London: George Bell and Sons, 1902), 246.
3. Quoted in *Our Angel Friends in Ministry and Song (Alfred Fowler, 1903)*, 5.
4. Ibid., 374.
5. From Spurgeon's sermon "God's Providence," published on October 15, 1908.
6. David Jeremiah, *What the Bible Says About Angels* (Sisters, OR: Multnomah Books, 1996), 22.
7. The Pentateuch is the name given to the first five books of the Bible.
8. Taken largely verbatim from a personal letter to the author from Terence Hammack, dated August 15, 2010.
9. Charles Hodge, *Systematic Theology, Vol. 1* (New York: Scribner Armstrong & Co, 1873), 638.

10. *The Familiar Discourses of Dr. Martin Luther*, translated by Captain Henry Bell (London: Baldwin, Craddock, and Joy, 1818), 316.

11. John Wesley, *Sermons on Several Occasions, Vol. 2* (New York: Carlton & Phillips, 1855), 134.

12. Quoted in *Our Angel Friends in Ministry and Song*, 46.

13. Based on conversations and subsequent e-mails from Dr. Mary Ruth Wisehart. Used with permission.

14. Wesley, *Sermons on Several Occasions, Vol. 2*, 137.

15. Merle Inniger, written by his wife, Gloria, as Merle passed away in 2006, and passed on to me by our mutual friend Warren Larson, director of the Zwemer Center for Muslim Studies at Columbia International University. The Innigers were missionaries to Pakistan. Used with permission.

16. From Martin Luther's hymn "A Mighty Fortress Is Our God," written in 1529 and translated from German by Frederic H. Hedge in 1853.

17. Quoted in *Our Angel Friends in Ministry and Song*, 57.

18. Norman Macleod, *Parish Papers* (New York: Robert Carter and Brothers, 1863), 123.

19. Quoted in *Our Angel Friends in Ministry and Song*, 60.

20. It's also possible that the star followed by the Magi was actually an angel who was leading them to the Christ child.

21. *The Ecclesiastical History of Socrates* (London: George Bell & Sons, 1892), 197.

22. Taken from a tract titled "Introducing Rev. Kenneth Ware of Paris, France," a transcript of a broadcast sermon on the ABC Network by C. M. Ward on April 19, 1959. Used by permission of Assemblies of God World Missions, with special thanks to Gloria Robinett, archivist.

23. Used with permission. You can read more about Mr. Qureshi in *The Peanut Butter Man* by R. W. Irwin, a missionary with The Evangelical Alliance Mission in Pakistan from 1956 to 1995. It's published by Tate Publishing & Enterprises, 2010.

24. Robert J. Morgan, *Real Stories for the Soul* (Nashville: Thomas Nelson, 2000), 249–251. Pieced together from several books and Internet articles about the *Titanic*. Lightoller's story also appeared in the Congressional Record of the investigation of the sinking of the Titanic. Lightoller lived until December 8, 1952. Interestingly, he was an adherent of the Christian Science faith.

25. Alida Stanwood, *Reinforcements* (New York: R. R. Beam & Co., 1915), 148.

26. Based on conversations and subsequent e-mails from Terry and Sue Hammack of SIM. Used with permission.

27. The verb in verse 9 is clearly a word for "sing." The verb in verses 12 and 13 is *lego*, which means to talk or communicate. It can mean either speak or sing, and since it's often used before portions in Revelation that are obviously poetical hymns, the NIV translators chose to use the word "sing."

28. Erwin W. Lutzer, *Hitler's Cross* (Chicago: Moody Press, 1995), 50, 61, 64.

29. C. Fred Dickason, *Angels: Elect and Evil* (Chicago: Moody Press, 1975), 162–163.

30. Wayne Grudem, *Systematic Theology* (Grand Rapids: Zondervan, 1994), 415.

31. Jan Winebrenner, *Steel in His Soul: The Dick Hillis Story* (Chicago: Moody Press, 1985), chap. 6.

32. Quoted by John Warner Barber in *An Account of the Most Important and Interesting Religious Events* (New Haven, CT: L.H. Young, 1834), 168–69.

33. Grudem, *Systematic Theology*, 427.

34. Corrie ten Boom, *Defeated Enemies* (Fort Washington, PA: Christian Literature Crusade, n.d.), 27.

35. Robert J. Morgan, *The Red Sea Rules* (Nashville: Thomas Nelson, 2001), 40.
36. J. Oswald Sanders, *Satan Is No Myth* (Chicago: Moody Press, 1975), 35–36.
37. Quoted by Frank L. Houghton in *Amy Carmichael of Dohnavur* (Fort Washington, PA: Christian Literature Crusade, 2000), 356.
38. Quoted by Robert J. Morgan in *Then Sings My Soul: Book 3* (Nashville: Thomas Nelson, 2011), 282.